THE CONNECTION SERIES

The Big Payback

*A Guide on Raising a Young Man as a Single Mother
from the Perspective of a Young Man*

Cederick W. Tardy II

**Cederick Tardy Enterprises
Houston, TX**

www.ctardyenterprises.com

Copyright ©2006 Cederick W. Tardy II

All rights reserved. No part of this publication may be reproduced, stored in a retrieval system or transmitted in any form or by any means, electronic, mechanical, photocopying, recording or otherwise, without the prior written permission of the publisher. No liability is assumed with respect to the use of the information contained herein. Neither is any liability assumed for damages resulting from the use of the information contained herein.

Library of Congress Control Number: 2006911133

ISBN-13: 978-0-9792301-0-3

ISBN-10: 0-9792301-0-1

Published by Cederick Tardy Enterprises, P.O. Box 840654, Houston, TX 77284

Note: This publication contains the opinions and ideas of its author. It is intended to provide helpful and informative material on the subject matter covered. It is sold with the understanding that the author and publisher are not engaged in rendering professional services in this book. If the reader requires special assistance in specific matters, a competent professional should be consulted.

The author and publisher specifically disclaim any responsibility for any liability, loss, or risk, personal or otherwise, which is incurred as a consequence, directly or indirectly, of the use and application of any of the contents of this book.

About The Author

Cederick W. Tardy is the author of *The Big Payback* and *A Head Start*. After living a life of drugs, sex, crime and pain, Cederick underwent an amazing transformation in his thinking and living. Through faith, trials, self-evaluation, and travel, he has truly developed as a young man. Cederick served in the United States Navy, attended college, operates Cederick Tardy Enterprises, and is currently writing a book titled: *What Father's Should be Telling Their Daughters*. Cederick has devoted his life to serving as a beacon to those battling the single mother's struggle.

I dedicate this book first to my Heavenly Father. Secondly, I dedicate this book to my mother and my grandmother who each fought the single mother's struggle. Lastly, I dedicate this book to all those who are fighting the struggle. I know you are taking a leap of faith. I thank you for your time, and I know your son will thank you too. This book is my payback to my mother, and my gift to you.

Introduction

Sometimes all we can do to help others is give our testimony and pray that they hear in it what they were supposed to hear.

- Cederick W. Tardy II

The Big Payback... The infamous youth written *parenting* book... What could it have to say? What could I have to say? What is my message? Two things my message is not. One, a gimmick. Two, bologna. My message is straightforward, plain, and truthful. My message is a blessing to some, an eye opener to a few, and just what the doctor ordered to the rest. My message is about life and the pursuit of a better one. Let me tell you how it all started.

It was 2004. I was sitting in a court building in a terrible state of affairs, heart pounding, scanning some disheartening paperwork. I was praying to God for an escape route, praying to God for a better way, praying to God for a way to keep my brother and sister out of the same predicaments I consistently found myself in.

As I have done for so many years, when I get nervous, when I get flustered, when life gets rough, I write. Two books that I've entitled, *The Connection Series*, are the product of what started in that building.

In my head, I was really just going to write letters to my mom about how I felt. I was going to let her know what I wish she would have done better when she was raising me. As I wrote I realized that she wasn't the only one to fault. *See, I had problems too.* With that in mind, I flipped the paper over and started writing to myself. I started writing everything I wish I had known back then that would have kept me out of so much trouble. Had I known back then what I know now, I would have been able to keep myself out of trouble.

We all know it is impossible to change the past, but we can change someone else's future by telling them what we have learned. I called my mother while I was sitting in that court building and told her what I was writing. I told her exactly what I was feeling. Her reply was, "You need to just write a whole book."

"A book?" I thought to myself. I didn't even read books back then so I laughed at her suggestion. How was I going to write a book if I don't read? She was serious though.

A few months later, my scraps and notes started to piece together into paragraphs and then chapters and then two separate books. It took over a year to finish writing, but every night as I stayed up well past two and three in the morning I knew it would all be worth it. My mother is the one who said I needed to share my

i

story . . . *our* story. She believed it would help a lot of people. All I can do is share my story . . . *our* story . . . and hope that she was right.

I can share the story of my, *our*, troubles and triumphs and the wisdom I, we, gained. I can share those things with you in hopes that you will be able to keep your son out of trouble. So, what is my message? "Learn from my mistakes. Learn from the mistakes my mother made. Learn to navigate the tricky road of single parenthood from the other side of the street." I may not be able to teach you everything, but trust me when I say that you will learn something.

What to expect

Most adults, especially single mothers, didn't know what to expect when I modestly expressed my initial idea of writing a *parenting book*. Most snubbed me and brushed me off, discrediting the very thought of my idea. But, there were a few who decided to take the time to hear me out. Those few learned a lot.

Unlike the traditional parenting book written by the 50-year-old, gray-haired psychologist, this message is not meant to be a parenting book at all; it is meant to be a "connections" book. The title, *The Connection Series*, signifies the uniting of the mother and son relationship through the principles of this series.

You and your son, who at this current moment may be so far apart, if you choose to take heed of what is written in these pages, will find yourselves connecting in the middle. Not just in the middle, but also at the top, connected, not by an umbilical chord, but by communication, love, and trust. Imagine shaking hands with your son at the top of a mountain and you can envision the goal of *The Connection Series*.

You can expect scores of analogies throughout this book, as well as several exercises that you will be asked to follow through with. These are by no means extraneous or strenuous exercises like some form of calisthenics. These exercises are simply things to do that will keep the relationship between you and your son fit and in shape. We all know that extended periods of physical exercise strengthen the muscles of the body, but the same thinking applies in the relationship you have with your son. Exercising the bonds in the relationship the two of you have will make the relationship stronger and much more capable of handling the weight and pressures that the teenage years bring.

Lastly, you can expect to hear a lot about how I grew up and the lifestyle I lived. I tell a lot about my life in hopes that through the things I went through you may glean some wisdom or sprout some ideas that will better your particular parenting situation. If you could just keep your kids from living the teenage life that I lived then it was all worth it.

If all I can do is say "this is how I did it," if it helps you, then let us both be thankful. Your situation may be similar, or it may be totally, completely, utterly, and drastically different from mine. Either way, just be patient. Remember that what may not help you was written because it will surely bless the life of another mother half way across the country reading this book at the same time you are. Your son may have never experienced a life of drugs, but another mother's son may be knee deep in cocaine and marijuana. Please be patient.

The Big Payback

The title of the first book of *The Connection Series* is *The Big Payback*. Short and simple, this book is my payback to my mother for all the hell, hurt, and horrors I put her through for most of my life. The Big Payback *is my way of telling my mother that I am sorry, and I value the sacrifices she made raising a child like me.* Tupac Shakur sang *Dear Mama*, but I had it on my heart to write a letter to my mother to show my gratitude. It just so happened that what I had to tell my mother would not only explain a lot to her, but also offer answers to many other mothers around the nation going through similar fiascoes.

The title of the second book of *The Connection Series* is *A Head Start*. *A Head Start* is really just what the title implies; it is a head start for your son. Lessons that I didn't learn until I was 20 years old have been written in plain English and placed right in his hands. All he has to do is read the book and he will have a head start on me, on his friends, on a lot of young men.

If I only touch one life, I pray that it is enough to cover the degree of sins I committed. *The Big Payback* and *A Head Start* are all about me reaching out and trying to help.

About me

Allow me to share with you a short biography of my life. I believe that this glimpse of the life I lived will show you why I am able to write this book. Additionally, I believe that this glimpse of the life I lived will excite you to change for the better before it is too late.

It is sad that only after a person hits rock bottom, do they find the strength and motivation to turn their life around for the better. That is exactly what happened with me. Born in Houston, Texas, in 1984, I spent 18 years of my life in and around that city causing a ruckus. I was by no means the worst kid in the world, but those close to me knew I was no angel.

My mother and father were married when I was born. We all lived together.

INTRODUCTION

My father and I fished a lot, and things were fine from what I can remember. Things were good until the second grade when my parents got divorced. When they got divorced it hit me like a ton of bricks. I did not understand what divorce was at that age, but I knew my parents were both asking me who I wanted to live with and all kinds of disturbing questions. They argued all the time, and I cried all the time. Divorce was a terrible thing, and I learned that in the second grade!

It was around the time of the divorce that my behavior turned sour. When I say sour, I mean sour. I began looking for attention everywhere because my father no longer lived with me, and my mother had to work long hours to provide the essentials for us. It is no shocking revelation, but I must point out that children need attention.

Depression kicked in for me at this time. I cried a lot. I cried about the divorce, about my father not being around, about everything. Depression had a hold on me early on, but in the 1980s, I do not think the idea of kids being depressed had as much validity as it does now. These days, it is okay for a kid to have a "condition" of some sort, but in the 1980s, I was just considered a crybaby.

My dad lived in a separate apartment, and he stayed active in my life when I was young. He coached my little league football team, he came to my choir events, he even continued to take me fishing. Things were not so bad with my parents being divorced until my mother decided to move to the suburbs, which was 40 minutes farther away from my father.

I began seeing less and less of my father. Since my mother had moved into a nicer neighborhood, I began seeing a lot less of her too. She had bigger bills to pay, which meant she had to spend more time at work. I felt abandoned. It seemed like I was the only kid who had a key to the house, cooked, cleaned, mowed the yard, and stayed home by himself until past 10 at night most nights. I was the only kid who did his own laundry, picked out his clothes for school, and made sure to be on the bus for school in the morning. I felt alone. *Independence had come WAY too fast, and with it came a whole lot of TROUBLE.*

My mother loved me. She was not trying to abandon me, but she had little time to nurture me and give me the attention I needed at that crucial age of my life. Many of life's lessons that I was supposed to learn from an adult I learned by spending hours and hours alone teaching myself. This lack of structure and supervision and training became my downfall. A child left to his or her own devices will find his or her way into a dismal situation.

The crybaby depression that I had as a preteen became a raging sadness as a young teen. I would express my despair with violent outbursts of aggression followed by severe bouts of loneliness and gloom. I wanted to talk, but no one was there for me to talk to.

I bottled all of my fears and frustrations inside of me, similar to taking a carbonated can and shaking it up violently. All it took from that point on was just one thing, one little thing, to open my top, and BAM it was all over! Depression was now an understatement; I was lost. *I had no role model, no guidance counselor, no real friends, no church, parents too busy, and most importantly, no Jesus.*
I was lost, but I bottled it all in, hardly telling anyone how I felt. I vented in poetry, volumes and volumes of poetry. By age 13, I was utterly lost and dead to the world. Depression had a hold on me so firmly that I became easily influenced by others, searching for some type of attention or sense of acceptance. I put my heart out to everyone, looking for acceptance. But misery loves company. I found myself tied into a group of friends that turned out to be the catalyst for destruction in my life. We all had problems. We all clung together, depressed, but bottled in.

Our inner conflicts began to evolve into outer conflicts. I started drinking at the age of *13*. Understand that I had drunk alcohol before and been drunk before the age of *13*, but what I mean is that I started *drinking*. I actually started buying alcohol and getting drunk on the weekends. Our social group started off slow, but whoever tells you that marijuana is the "gateway drug" for teenagers is misleading you. The "gateway drug" is whatever starts the addict on his path to becoming an addict, and alcohol is a drug. At 13, I started drinking and smoking weed. Nothing too harmful, right? I was just a kid, having fun, experimenting, right?

The weed and alcohol evolved into a multitude of pills, then LSD (acid), Ecstasy (X), cocaine, methamphetamines, inhalants, mushrooms, over-the-counter drugs, and whatever else could get me out of the harsh reality of being independent at an early age. Added to this were violent acts of vandalism, skipping school, and even more extreme substance abuse. Most of the drugs I did, I did while at school, or at least I bought them at school or through someone from school. I believe I may have held the unofficial record for coming to school high the most consecutive days. Months and months would go by without me spending one day sober.

After school, I hung out with petty drug dealers, tried selling drugs myself, and smoked as much weed as possible. I sold what pills and weed I could to support my habit. Many times the drugs clouded my mind and caused suicidal thoughts to take over my soul. "I want out!" my heart would cry loudly to my head. Oh boy, it was as if my bones were trying to escape my muscle tissue. It honestly felt like there was something evil inside me. Many times, I would sit and stare at the shotgun I had been given one Christmas, thinking it might possibly be my way out. I can remember staring down the barrel with my finger nearing the trigger.

Things got low for me. I never pulled the trigger, but God knows I did try to take myself out many times. The closest incident involved inhalants. In case you are unfamiliar with inhalants, they are any chemical that you can inhale that gives you a rapid high. The favorites of our bunch were CO_2 canisters, street-named Whippets, and Freon, which is the agent used in refrigerators and air conditioners. One night I tried to kill myself by inhaling an excessive amount of Freon at a friend's house, surrounded by my peers. None of them knew I was trying to kill myself, and honestly, I did not know or care.

I fought with loneliness and depression for most of my life. By the age of 16, I was kicked out of my mother's house for the first time, which changed my whole outlook on life. I ended up moving to my father's house, but he had a wife and a new child already. I was forced, actually I forced myself, to stay sober. I knew my life was getting out of hand. I knew I was throwing away the potential I had.

When I went to my dad's house a lot of things changed, including the high school I would be going to. I spent one semester at a new high school and I spent that entire semester as a hermit. The boy who used to get in trouble daily for talking in class was now a recluse. Could you imagine a kid going to school every day with his headphones on, listening and writing poetry in his notepad? Parents, sudden behavior changes of any kind need to be addressed.

I did not say many words that entire semester. I did not make one friend, and if I held a conversation, it was not by choice. At that point in time I learned that I could count on myself to be my support system if need be. I grew up a lot. But how many of us know that *until an element is taken out of its environment and given enough time to completely evolve, it will quickly reform back to its old makeup once placed back into its original environment?*

During that semester at my dad's house I grew into my own being, found myself, and realized I did not need to strive for the affection of others to be complete. Knowing who I was and what I wanted completed me. That confidence only lasted as long as I was away from my old environment though. The next school year started with me right back at my mother's house, around my same old friends, doing the same old dirt, but this time even worse.

Things got way out of hand. I usually did whatever I wanted to do. Friends would come over to the house after school and get high with me while my mother was at work. I would sell drugs out of the front yard. One day I even had the balls to smoke weed in the house, with my mom at home asleep in her room!

That same night I ran away to Louisiana for nearly a week. I left with $256, two friends, a pound of marijuana, a few Ecstasy pills, and a dream of turning that into some real money. Well... that didn't work out because as I said, I was only gone for about a week. Things needed to change, because my life was going down like a kite on a windless day. I had already gotten alcohol poisoning, nearly committed suicide, crashed my car causing damage to my left eye, almost hit by a train, arrested a few times and the list goes on.

I wanted better, but I just could not get better going in my life like so many other young people. My mother was so awesome though, because she never gave up on me. She kept dragging me to church. She kept dragging me to church even though I was drunk, even though I was high, even though I would throw up in the church bathroom because I was hung over, even though I was making funny faces at the preacher, even though, even though, even though... She never gave up. Even though I had just run away to Louisiana, she never gave up. Even though to infinity, she never gave up.

I made up my mind that I was not going to college. Truthfully, I talked myself out of college. I was going to graduate at 17, and I just "knew" I was way too young and way too impressionable to attempt going to college. My theory: Why spend thousands of dollars for me to fail? No self-confidence. Instead of college, I was going to join the Air Force. Graduation day came, and surprisingly, I passed. Thank God I graduated on time, because another year at that school, in that city, in that environment, may have done me in.

I stopped smoking weed a few days after I graduated high school and signed up for the Air Force. Everyone in my family was so proud of me, and thankful to see me clear-eyed. Things were looking up for me. Notice the word were.

A few weeks after I had signed up and taken the urinalysis, I received a letter from the U.S. Air Force that read, "Due to the high amount of THC found in your urine you are no longer able to join the ranks of the U.S. Air Force." My whole world, my parent's whole world, and everyone that knew me were crushed. The U.S. Air Force was all I had planned. So there I was flat on my face, again.

What else could I do? I did not take the SAT, ACT, or even turn in one application for college. My only plan was scratched from the drawing board upon the arrival of that letter. I cried. My father and mother cried. What was I going to do?

I tried community college, but since I slept my way through high school, my placement test scores were beyond low. *My family as a whole had no idea what to do because we had never planned for my future.* It was as if we were staring at the Pacific Ocean with only a dingy. We did not know how we were going to get past this obstacle. If only we had planned. I grabbed my Bible and I started reading it for some reason. I think I was upset with God and looking for some answers. I started reading that book until I could not read anymore.

As it turned out, the Air Force recruiter went to my church. After a Bible study, he asked me if I was still interested in the military. I said yes. He told me that if I was able to stay off drugs, I should look into joining the Marines, Army, or the Navy. My stepfather was in the Army during Desert Storm and my best friend had joined the Marines after September 11th. Neither of them was encouraging me to

Introduction

join either branch, so I decided to try the Navy. I wanted to travel. I wanted to leave Houston. I remember I told my grandmother, "I am tired of watching the sun set over Houston."

I spent seven months waiting to get into the Navy, and in those seven months I busted my butt training for boot camp. I shaved my head. I stayed sober. I volunteered at my church and even held a job at McDonald's. I was determined to do whatever it took to ensure I stayed sober.

January 14, 2003, finally came around, and I started down the path to my adult life, the path that would eventually lead me to writing this book. The Navy took me in, clothed me, fed me, gave me plenty of opportunities, and even made me a military police officer, which my old friends got a BIG kick out of. Many of the things I learned through being a "cop" I share throughout this book. By the time I turned 19, I had traveled to Hawaii, Australia, Guam, Dubai, Singapore, Mexico, and a host of other countries. I called my grandmother just to tell her that I had seen the sun set somewhere else other than Houston. I had watched it set over the coast of Africa.

Do not get your hopes up just yet. I still got into a lot of trouble in the Navy. I had a hard time with authority since I was used to answering mainly to myself. I do not tell you this to ruin the story, but to reinforce the fact that *there is always hope*. No matter how many mistakes we make, the story is not finished until we take our last breath. I got arrested for vandalism after only five months in the Navy. Fresh out of military police officer's school, I sat in jail for two days before posting bail, facing seven felony charges. It took years of hard work and tons of prayer to get me right.

It took dedication and perseverance from many people to get me in line. It was not until I moved to San Diego and saw how people in California lived, the cars they drove, the food they ate, and even the dogs they owned, that I realized there was more to life than trying to be cool, drinking, and eating fried chicken. It finally clicked that if I wanted what they had I was going to have to start doing what they were doing. That was the breakthrough I needed. Things finally began looking up for me.

The boy who was once laughed at after taking his placement scores at a community college was now attending college while serving his country in the Navy. The boy who was once a rotten scoundrel was now attending church regularly and volunteering in a youth organization in an attempt to be a role model. Quickly my life turned around. I went from not knowing how to save a penny to having investments, multiple savings accounts, and a five-figure bank account on a petty military salary. Here I am now, writing to mothers, writing to young men. Rarely does a person's life turn around so drastically so quickly. Like my mom said, I had to tell my story. What could I have to say?

Believe me, I have a lot to say. I have learned from my past, and I believe that anyone who is open-minded will be able to learn from my past, not because I am someone special, but because what is in your hands is something special. What you are holding is not your ordinary parenting book, but is instead a real life account and real life tips that will positively alter the way your family operates. Even if you only learn one thing or change one thing for the better in your family after reading this book, you will have become a better person. My motto is, *"Learn what you can from whoever is willing and capable to teach you."*

There is hope for you, mom, and hope for your son. Whether your son is 11 years old and not yet in his terrible teens, or whether you have a ferocious teenager living in the room across the hall, there is hope. If there was hope and not only hope but also a way for me, there is hope and a way for you and your son. And guess what? You have what my mother and I never had; you have solid advice.

Similar to a lookout on the top of a ship, the guy who tells the helmsman which way to steer the ship to avoid running it aground, you have me, your "lookout" if you will. My sole goal in life is to help keep as many youths and parents as I can from running aground. Let me be your lighthouse on the rocky shore shining in the late hours, warning you of danger ahead when you are headed in the wrong direction.

I have traveled in the wrong direction before. Ask my mother; we have been there before. My beacon is bright and my cry is loud. Listen to what this book has to say. Check your heart carefully. Examine yourself fully. Do not casually read this book as you would any other, believing you have heard all of this before, or that you are above my mental faculty. I could not tell you where to go or what to avoid unless I have first been to that place myself and learned of the perils that await the unsuspecting. When someone asks you why you would listen to a youngster about parenting, tell that person, "Because he has been there before, and I do not want my child going where he went."

This book is a beacon of encouragement and warning to all those who are raising young men in this day and age.

In this book, you will read numerous chapters written by me, and one written by my mother. I believe it was important for her to share her account. Just having my mother writing a chapter is obvious that she approves of what is written here in your hands, and she believes it can be helpful to you.

Additionally, in this book you will notice sentences that are written in italics. These sentences are sentences I felt to be notable statements or simply statements that needed to be emphasized.

Read these over a few times slowly to ensure comprehension. *Until there is*

Introduction

comprehension, there will never be revelation, and until there is revelation, there will never be a change of heart.

All I want to do is help. All I want to do is make a difference in the world. If only one kid's life is positively affected by the words I have written, then all my hard work and dedication were not in vain.

Lastly, before you journey through *The Big Payback*, I ask that every single time you open this book you do so with a pen and paper nearby to capture your own thoughts and ideas. The ideas that will come to you will be better ways for you to raise your child, questions that I may have left unanswered, or insight that may be beneficial to another single mother. When you happen to write down something that you know will benefit my growth, be kind enough to let me know about it. At the end of the book you will find my personal e-mail address and mailing address where I will be accepting messages.

Take notes. Write in your book. Make it personal. If you are ready, let's get started with chapter one. It is from my mother.

Table of Contents

Ch. 1: Never Give Up On your Son 1
Ch. 2: You Don't Have the Right to Give Up 7
Ch. 3: Nature's Moms 11
Ch. 4: Six Barriers to Effective Listening and
       Six Tips for Effective Listening 15
Ch. 5: Actions Speak Louder Than Words......................................25
Ch. 6: Avoid Discouragement 33
Ch. 7: Taking the Reigns and Being the Leader as a Mother 39
Ch. 8: Rebuilding Lost Trust 45
Ch. 9: How to Be and Stay in Control 51
Ch. 10: Once You Have Him...57
Ch. 11: Clams and Clam Openers...63
Ch. 12: Just Give Him a Toy and He Will Be Fine.........................73
Ch. 13: Overcoming a Single Mother's Financial Struggles.........77
Ch. 14: Parental Teamwork 85
Ch. 15: Planning Ahead 89
Ch. 16: The Power of God's Word 97
Ch. 17: Do You Put Off Until Tomorrow What
        Should Have Been Done Yesterday? 103
Ch. 18: Just Some Thoughts..107
Ch. 19: Stop Fighting With Your Son and Teach Him 109
Ch. 20: Suicide 115
Ch. 21: The Boy's Father 123
Ch. 22: The Difference Between Working Hard in the Family and
        Working Hard for the Family 129
Ch. 23: The Greatest Compliments Come From Your Son 137
Ch. 24: Television and Other Influences: The Affects
        They Have on Your Son's Personality.................................143
Ch. 25: Vision Chapter...147
Ch. 26: You Have to Believe 151
Conclusion...159
Connection Questions 160
Epilogue 161
Promotion Page 163

Chapter One

Never Give Up on Your Son

Children need and want boundaries. They need consistency; they need us to set an above-average example that they can aspire to become. We owe it to them as parents.

- Margo Williams Handy

As Cederick's mother, this chapter is a difficult one for me to write because the wounds have not yet scabbed over and the memories are still very fresh.

Even today, two years after his felony arrest, I stiffen when Cederick is home on Navy leave and asks to use the car. Cederick's four high school years were sheer hell in our home. My husband (Cederick's stepfather) and I would brace ourselves each weekend for the inevitable–a car accident, a call from the police station, a call from Cederick saying he wasn't coming home (and that was before things turned really bad), and then afterwards–no call at all, just sleepless nights wondering if he was dead or alive. We felt like prisoners in our own home.

The work you are about to read is nothing short of amazing. Not only because the author is my son and I'm so very proud of him, but also because this is parenting information from a son's perspective. I wish this series had been written before my son's birth. Then I would have known what was going on in the recesses of Cederick's mind. With this knowledge, perhaps I would not have remained ignorant and in denial for so long. But, it's not too late for you.

My message to all mothers is to never give up on your child. *The road may be long, bumpy, and full of what seem to be dead ends, but never, ever give up.*

You may be saying that your child is not too bad. He may get good grades, does not drink or use drugs, and is respectful most of the time. And, as a single mother, you may be doing your best to keep clothes on his back, food on the table, and spend quality time with him when you're not dog tired.

Or, perhaps your son is on a far worse journey than Cederick's. Your son may be in a gang, in jail, or he may be stealing from your household to fund his drug habit.

It could be that your son is somewhere in between. The scary thing is, before I came out of my haze of denial, I thought scenario number one perfectly described our home life.

Never Give Up

Before I share the courses of action Cederick's stepfather and I took to help guide our son, I'll share my side of the *Cederick Tardy Story*. I don't mean to say I have my side and Cederick has his. A better choice of words would be *perspective*. We each had our own perspectives, which ran parallel and never connected back then.

From my perspective, my son was born with above-average intelligence and potential. He was bright-eyed and could hold a bottle from the day he was born. Just days old, he would scour the room looking at everything and everyone in it, seemingly studying it all. He is no different today. He seemed to come out of the womb talking. For as long as I can remember, Cederick talked, asked questions, talked, and talked some more. Until just after the divorce.

Like most mothers who seek divorce, I thought I was doing what was best for Cederick. No longer did he have to listen to the arguments, be pitted one against the other, or watch me lose myself as I tried to live with someone who was verbally, spiritually, and mentally abusive. In reality, the divorce was best for *me*. Sure, in the long run it was probably the right thing to do for everyone involved, but looking back, as parents, we should have been far more aware of how Cederick was going to react to his little world being turned upside down.

After the divorce, Cederick began to slowly drift within himself. It was barely noticeable at first and I can only see it now looking back. At the time, I was so self-absorbed. Following the divorce, I felt scared and numb.

Normal is something I tried to create after the divorce. Cederick and I had buddy dinners; I read to him, and helped him with homework. We even moved to the suburbs and out of apartment living. I was determined to give Cederick a good life. Looking back, the move was one more thing that alienated Cederick. It took him away from the school district he had known most of his life, away from his best friend, and farther away from his father.

At that time, Cederick's slow slippage into his cave became more obvious, and he also hated me. He wouldn't hug me and rarely talked to me. If we did speak, within seconds the conversation would escalate into an argument. One day I received an investigatory call from Cederick's school. Cederick told his teacher that he hadn't eaten in days. Maybe Cederick thought he would be taken away from me to live with his father, or maybe it was a way to get back at me if he told a lie that would get me in real trouble, or perhaps it was another cry for attention. I never asked his intent.

I knew things were getting bad, but I rationalized it away by telling myself: he would grow out of it, he was entering the crazy teenage years, if his Dad would spend more time with him he'd be better, if only... if only. Meanwhile, I worked long hours trying to get ahead in corporate America and also to pay the mortgage.

Cederick spent a lot of time alone. But, I had spent time alone a lot as a child, and I turned out alright, didn't I? That was my thinking back then.

As a preteen, Cederick was quiet with bursts of anger, disruptive in school, his grades could range from straight As to Cs and Ds, and his writings were progressively dark. I sought psychological help based on the content of his poems. Cederick fooled the first couple of counselors. They were impressed with his demeanor, intelligence, and ability to answer the psychological test questions correctly. My son was always very clever in telling people what they wanted to hear to get out of uncomfortable situations. Each counselor released Cederick saying he was "cured." I knew better. I also knew what was really bothering Cederick, but I could never be the one to bring the real issue to light. That had to come from Cederick.

When my son was in his preteen years, I remarried a wonderful man. Unlike other boyfriends, my son admired James and listened to him, even though he could be *very* long winded. James is also to be awarded a few gold stars. Very few men would have knowingly walked into a time bomb. James was one of the first people to tell me, *"Don't give up on your son."* Marrying James was the first right thing I did where Cederick's transformation was concerned. Of course, I didn't know this at the time.

I ignored Cederick's first two years of drug use. I was in denial about my smart, handsome little boy. My mind recognized the symptoms, but my heart said that his blank gaze and watery eyes were caused by bad allergies, his mood swings were due to teen hormones, and his growing disrespect came from outside influences disguised as friends. After all, how could he be on drugs? He was meticulous about his hygiene, clothing, and appearance, continued to get decent grades, and I could see glimpses of the intelligent boy I knew was in there since the first day I laid eyes on him as a newborn.

Even at this stage in his drug usage, he watched the *Discovery Channel*, the *History Channel*, and could tell you anything about any species of animal. He wanted to be a veterinarian. That is, until we took him on a field trip to Texas A&M and the tour guide talked him right out of that dream. She said it was harder to be a veterinarian than a doctor. I didn't realize it at that time, but Cederick's self-esteem was very low. He didn't believe he was smart and, therefore, the college option was shot down in this one day, in his mind.

Toward the end of the 10th grade, I finally admitted to myself and to my husband that Cederick was using drugs. As I mentioned, it was not extremely noticeable. But, I knew my son wasn't "my son." He was a child on drugs and was taking on the personality of the drugs. He lost all interest in extracurricular activities, he went out with his friends, ate, slept and was increasingly paranoid, believing I and everyone else was out to get him.

Our faith in God really began to strengthen during this time. The three of us had received salvation. It seemed Cederick began to get worse the day after he accepted salvation. James and I prayed, and would even try to pray with Cederick. No matter how drunk or high he was, or what hour he came in, we always dragged him to church. And, if Cederick came in after we left for church, he had to listen to the tape and write a report. By the way, our form of discipline since Cederick was very young was to insist that he write a report regarding his behavior and what he could have done differently. Little did we know, we were helping to hone his writing skills.

From the 10th to the 12th grade, life was a blur for me. It was a never-ending battle of wills. James and I refused to give up on Cederick. Well-meaning friends would tell me that Cederick was going to do what he was going to do, and that he was at an age where I had no control. Others said he'd grow out of it. And the parenting books I read said parents should not impose their expectations on their children.

In my view, if I took any other course of action but to stay on Cederick's butt, I was giving up on his potential. Children, whether they are five or 15 years old, do not have the ability to guide and direct themselves; they need our guidance. And, I was convinced Cederick wanted better for himself. Most of all, we knew God had a purpose for him. We didn't push Cederick to be a doctor, lawyer, or any particular profession. We just wanted him to be happy and to make a living doing anything positive and legal.

At this time, we knew three things: Cederick was not going to use drugs while living in our household. He was going to church whether he liked it or not. Furthermore, refusing to finish high school was not an option. And then, the real hell began.

For the next two years, Cederick's behavior worsened. Most days, I didn't recognize him. He even began looking less boyish; haggard, and old. The whites of his eyes were yellow. On some days, he looked downright ugly. It wasn't until just recently that I knew the extent of his drug and alcohol addiction. This is about as far as I'll go into the spiral that Cederick ventured on. Cederick will tell his story in the chapters to come.

Moms, children are very good at disguising their drug usage. *Visine* is their friend. If they are too hung over, they get a hankering to "spend the night at a friend's house." They don't look like the average junkie we see portrayed in the movies.

I can say that it was around the 11th grade that my husband and I finally found the wisdom we needed to help Cederick out of his hell.

Our church, New Light Christian Center Church in Houston, has a teaching series on raising difficult children. I wish I'd learned about it earlier. James and I applied every principle on that tape, to the letter. The first thing we learned was to set a proper example. Our children mimic what they see. So, we took away all excuses from Cederick. No longer could he say he drank because we drank. James and I stopped drinking alcohol. No beers while watching football and no glasses of wine with an elegant dinner.

Next, we established rules but, this time, we enforced them. Cederick had a curfew, he was to keep his grades up, do his chores around the home, attend church, and he was not to use drugs–period. There was zero tolerance. If the rules were broken, he had to leave the home.

When the time came that I had to ask Cederick to leave because of his drug use, it was the absolute hardest thing I had ever done in my life. It was gut wrenching and I cried endlessly after he left. My heart was broken. Even though I had fallen into a depression after Cederick left to live with his father, I knew it was crazy for us to expect a different result and continue to do the same things we were doing. We loved Cederick enough to not enable his conduct.

We had to set boundaries and consistently live by them. Children need and want boundaries. They need consistency; they need us to set an above average example they can aspire to. We owe it to them as parents.

To abide by the rules, I had to forgive myself for any prior guilt due to not always giving Cederick the proper attention and guidance he needed. Cederick would always yell at me saying, "It is too late to start being a parent now!" I had to close my ears to that and just believe the principles would work. James and I didn't have a choice. Cederick was either headed to jail, or to the grave, or he would become a member of the living dead who hang out on the street corners. Some of you may need to get beyond the guilt and shame you feel due to your own prior drug use, or wild ways of life as a younger person. It's important that your child see that change is possible, no matter what you've done in the past. If they can't see it in you, how can they believe it for themselves?

Even when Cederick lived with his father, we continued to call, visit, and guide him. We also arranged for him to see another counselor. This one was different. She saw beneath Cederick's veil. After several sessions, she uncovered the truth of Cederick's depression. In addition to being upset with me over divorcing his father, Cederick had grown to understand that he was also disappointed with his father's inability to be physically and mentally available to him. This was the breakthrough Cederick needed to begin living in truth.

It was just the beginning, however, and even after Cederick returned home, it was hell. After some time, Cederick was asked to leave the home for the second and third time due to drug use.

One day at church, the pastor's wife, Dr. Bridget Hilliard, was teaching a lesson on raising difficult children. At the conclusion, she suggested sowing a seed for a changed behavior in our child. So, that's what I did. I don't recall the amount of money sowed; I only remember that it was significant for me at the time. For those who may be unfamiliar with the term sowing, it is a biblical principle taught at some churches that refers to making a financial sacrifice in the belief that God will see your sacrifice and move on your behalf. It takes faith, just as any other Christian principle takes faith.

Dr. Bridget also suggested writing a specific confession and saying it daily. We developed a confession of faith for Cederick's deliverance. I memorized the confession and said it daily and sometimes two or three times a day. Whenever I felt fear gripping me, I said that confession. When Cederick came on my heart stronger at sometimes than others, I said that confession. And, when I didn't know where he was or what he was doing, I said that confession. Not long after this, Cederick learned he had not been accepted by the Air Force. This was the beginning of the transformation. The parenting, praying, and confessions continue to this day. Only now, it's somewhat out of "maintenance."

Today, I counsel mothers to never choose a career over their children's welfare. I've learned from reading my son's series, the child's perception is that work takes precedence over them. In turn, the child internalizes that to mean they are not worthy of your time and therefore are not worthy individuals. The worst thing we can do as parents is to damage our child's self-worth. Sure, we have to work. But, do we have to work the overtime? Must we take that promotion at this time? Is climbing the ladder more important than raising our children?

Sometimes, it is not work that we choose over our child. Sometimes, it's time we spend doing anything else that keeps us away from our children and the home. Even though I always told Cederick he was smart, could do anything, and was handsome, his perception of my actions was that work was more important than he was. Cederick needed to know when it was his time to be with me so that he could always count on that. I didn't realize the significance of that back then.

Moms, please have the courage to continue reading this book, the tenacity to never give up on your child, and the foresight to see and nurture the potential in your child that they may not yet see in themselves. It's never too late.

Chapter Two

You Don't Have the Right to Give Up

Sometimes I wonder why my mother never gave up on me, but then I remember that a mother would never give up on her child.

- Cederick W. Tardy II

    Mothers, it's up to you. Set principles for your life and abide by those principles. Set principles for your son and guide him into living by those principles. You are the leader.
    Can you remember how you used to play tug of war as a kid? Can you remember how hard you fought to win? Do you remember how you would get a good stance, dig down deep into the earth, and then pull with everything you had? You did not want to let the other team win. You did not want to give up the fight. You fought with everything you had in order to keep the opposition from taking the rope that was yours.
    That, mothers, is exactly how you have to fight for your son. You have to dig down deep, get a good stance, and fight!
    After reading my version of the *Cederick Tardy Story*, and my mother's, you should understand that the absolute last thing you can do as a mother is give up on your son. No matter how rough things look, don't throw in the towel.
    My mother is the one with the testimony to tell. I am only the result of her not giving up on me no matter how much she may have wanted to. One day I hope she writes a book bearing this title. My mother truly believes you have to make up your mind early on that you cannot give up on your son. She says it is much more than a verbal statement, but a resolve, a state of mind.
    My mother somehow did not give up on me. She says that she would have if not for various people telling her not to give up on me. I know in her position I would have been tempted to quit. I was holding her back from her dreams. I was holding her back from her financial freedom. I was holding her back from everything, and all I was giving her was pain. I know many of you may think you have the worst kid in the world, but you do not.
    I was not the worst kid in the world either, even though I was pretty close. I could have at least gotten a bronze medal. I was a liar, thief, cheater, scammer,

vandal, actor, drug addict, putrid-mouthed little punk kid who had no respect for most people and no real will to live.

Believe me, my mom had it bad. But she did not have the worst kid. Do you remember back when "Scared Straight" was a big rage intended to keep kids from landing in prison? Do you remember how it worked? They would take kids to a prison, give them a long briefing, and then walk them through the prison. It was almost like going to a zoo to see the animals in cages. Instead of animals, these were grown men, images of where those young kids' lives could end if they didn't straighten up. I suggest this to you; try this same type of awakening experience, but with yourself.

Go to a juvenile detention center and ask if you could walk the grounds to see the kids behind bars. Find out stories about some of the kids. Why, you ask? Because those are some of the worst kids in the world! Your boy is probably at home right now playing video games even though you told him to clean up. Really horrible, huh? No! What is horrible is the 12-year-old kid who murdered his parents or neighbors. What is bad is that child who was starting fires all over the city, or those two kids who shot up that school. Your kid is not that bad, most likely.

That is the whole idea. Before you give up, realize that your child is not that bad. He may disobey you every time you ask him to do something, but at least he hasn't killed you or sold everything in your house for crack! The point of the visit, and even if you do not go but visualize the juveniles behind bars, is to remind you of the fact that your child is not that bad.

You have to appreciate him for his good qualities and stop looking at the negatives all of the time.

Despite my deficiencies, my mother didn't give up on me. She stuck around and defended me even when it was costing her her own life to keep me alive. She loved me too much to give up on me, and I know she is the only "physical" reason I am here right now.

She had plenty of chances to give up on me. She could have given up on me when I ran away from home to Louisiana to sell drugs. After all, I was doing illegal stuff, I missed Thanksgiving, a week of school, I had just been busted by her for smoking weed in my own room while she was in the house, and worst of all, I missed her birthday. All that happened in the span of a week, and that week's span resembled many other weeks.

She could have given up on me when I got suspended from school for fighting. She could have given up when she got my report cards and saw how many days of school I had missed even though I told her I was at school. She could have given up on me when my stepfather caught my best friend and I drinking beers in the house in ninth grade. She could have given up on me when I was yelling at her, wishing I could fight her. She could have given up when I was sitting in the corner rocking back and forth with a crazy look on my face. She could have given up after the time she and my stepdad yelled at me and I went and got my shotgun and began cleaning it in the living room as a show of force. She could have given up on me when I tried to fight my stepfather. She could have given up on me when I got arrested and was brought home sloppy drunk, covered in alcohol, and covered in vomit at age 15. She could have given up on me when I got arrested at 16. She could have given up on me when I caught seven felonies at 18.

She could have given up on me when she found out I had been busted by my dad with half an ounce of Hydro marijuana, pipes, and the rest of my drug paraphernalia. She could have given up on me when I told her she was the worst mom in the world and I hated her guts. She could have given up on me when I crashed my car in a ditch after drinking all night with my friends and severely damaged my left eye. Instead, she got me glasses so I could see again. She could have given up on me when I crashed my car again driving high off marijuana. She could have given up on me when I was asking for 20 bucks every two days for lunch money when really I was spending it on weed. She could have given up on me when all her alcohol kept winding up missing. Instead, she decided to quit drinking for my benefit. She could have given up on me so many more times, but for the sake of your reading, I will stop here.

She had more than enough reasons to give in and give up, but she didn't. She loved me and did her best to guide me through it all. She tried her best. She tried so hard to provide for me when I was young, but I took it for granted and pissed many years of my life away trying to live the life I had seen on the movies. What movies? *Boys in the Hood, Good Fellas, Scarface, Fear and Loathing in Las Vegas, Half Baked*, et cetera.

As a sidebar, I recommend that you start watching anything your child might be influenced by and then listen up for your child acting out those scenes and lines from the movies. Even do the same with his music. This is crucially important to understanding who he is. I believe that once you get to really know who he is, and not just who you think he is, then you cannot help but love him even more. The more you learn about and get to know your son, the more you will learn to appreciate him.

Back to the main message, just imagine what would have happened had my mother turned her back on me. Even through my hard times while in the military she didn't give up on me. Instead she kept in touch. She gave me advice when I needed it. She was always there for me. She never gave up and I have to respect her for that. She sacrificed for me. Even when it was holding her back, she sacrificed for me. It seemed like as soon as I left home she started her own business, bought a new house, and her marriage got much stronger. I know I was holding her back, but she hung in there to make sure I was going to be all right before she took care of herself.

There is never going to be another mother for your son. No one will ever be able to love him in the same way that you can love him. And since you are his mom, if you do not love him, most likely he will not love himself. If you give up on him, he will give up on himself. If you do not support him, he will not support himself.

But if you love him, he will love you. His love for you will be his reason to live, straighten up, and fly right. You are everything he needs to be successful. Yes, you are everything he needs to start off in life. You are his shield from destruction. You are his protection, his wisdom, his life, his love, and his peace when things get rough. You are his mother. Do not give up on your son; he is not that bad.

Chapter Three

Nature's Moms

You can learn things in the strangest places; all you have to do is look.
— Cederick W. Tardy II

I am a nature nut. I love watching animals. Cute ones and ugly ones, it does not matter to me. I like animals because they are pure in their behaviors. For this reason, I like to look at nature and nature's laws and analyze them against our own human ways of living. I have noticed many things. I have noticed that nature is both cruel and gentle, unforgiving yet so very patient. Nature never entirely destroys the environment as we humans do.

Humans create bulldozers, explosives, and pollution. We destroy the earth, but nature understands how to put everything in its proper place. Even when it may seem nature is destroying itself, it is all an ingenious plan of regeneration.

Mother Nature regenerates itself with things like forest fires, volcanoes, and earthquakes. They may seem catastrophic to our feeble brains, but nature knows how to fix itself. Volcanoes build new land masses, and earthquakes release tension in the tectonic plates. Forest fires clear out old vegetation and make it possible for the new undergrowth to get an adequate amount of sunlight. Nature is perfect.

I believe we can learn a lot of our parenting techniques from nature. In nature we find excellent parental examples, like the elephant and even the octopus. These mothers put their own lives in jeopardy in order to protect their offspring. The elephant parenting style is to guide their young, and lead by example. They teach their kids what food to eat, how to use their trunks to gather herbs and nuts, all by way of example. They also teach their children to use their trunks for bathing and drinking. Elephants teach their children how to dig for water in the dry season, and how to strip tree bark when food is scarce, and they do it all by example.

These are just a few examples of how elephants teach their children everything they possibly can so that they can survive in the harsh world. If only every human parent taught their kids everything they needed to learn in order to survive. Most human parents choose to let their kids wander off and figure stuff out on their own. A child left to his own devices is a disaster waiting to happen. If a young elephant were left to fend for its own in the wilderness, even if only from 9 a.m. to 5 p.m., it would be slaughtered by its ravenous environment. The same is true with human young. A baby elephant left to fend for itself would be hunted down by ferocious predators; lions and hyenas would make short work of the baby.

In the human world we have predators too. Sexual predators or any evil person can make short work of a child left to his own discretion.

When a herd of elephants is faced with a conflict, such as a pride of lions, the adult elephants will put their own bodies in the way of danger to protect their young. The elephants will surround the young with their backsides in and their mighty front sides facing the threat. Elephants learn to cooperate as a team; all the mothers work together moving in ranks and if need be they will stomp any force that gets in their way.

Not even a strong pride of lions has a chance of killing a baby elephant when it is properly guarded. The mother puts her life on the line for her child. The elephant mother fights to protect her calf from danger without any consideration on whether it will cost her her life. The same type of protective mothering also belongs to the octopus.

You may be thinking, "Why is the guy telling me to raise my kids like an octopus?" You can learn things from the strangest places if you only look. The octopus mother is one of the most selfless and faithful of all mothers on the earth. Once she has her babies, she takes on an unspoken vow to protect them from danger. Their danger comes from the codfish, a ferocious predator.

These fish hang around the nest sites of the female octopus waiting eagerly for her to leave, and then they ravish the nestlings, devouring all of the eggs. It is the defense that this mother uses to defend her offspring from this threat that makes the female octopus so great. She will wait around the entire time her eggs are forming, until they burst alive with new octopi. She will forego eating and caring for herself for weeks, fending off every predator she can from eating her babies.

This is not like the human parents who give up on their kids when things look rough.

No, the octopus goes for weeks without food, and tirelessly defends her children day and night. This defense ends up costing the mother octopus her very life. The female octopus dies shortly after the babies have hatched due to malnourishment and exhaustion. Not only does she die, but the predators she fought away for weeks now have their chance to get their fill on her dead body. As the predators feed on her dead body, her babies escape into the dark ocean. Sad way to go, but her legacy lives on in her young. She sacrifices everything, even her own existence, for her kids. How many human parents these days do such a thing?

Take some time to sit down and watch *Animal Planet* or the *Discovery Channel*, and watch how even the mother pig cares for her babies with her whole heart.

THE BIG PAYBACK

Where do we humans go wrong as parents? Do we get lost in the rat race of work, sleep, work and sleep? Are we so worried about the next bill that we forget about little Bill, Johnny, Chris, or Tommy in the other room playing video games confused about his future, doing almost anything to fit in?

Let's look at a few things that nature showed us in these examples. We will start with the octopus since it is fresh on our minds. I have one big question: Where are the fathers? Did you not notice that the female octopus was defending her young, raising them, and sacrificing her life? It is as if the male doesn't know that the female needs help.

This is not a father-bashing book, but look at what not having a father around has done to the octopus family. The mother octopus has taken on so many roles that she has physically worn herself out and died prematurely. This is similar to a human mother who works two or three jobs to make ends meet. She works so hard that by the end of the day she has tired herself out. She has no energy to go home and teach her kids anything because she has to go to work the next morning. Now her kids are left up to their own judgment, walking the streets alone with no guidance, similar to the octopus babies who have to defend themselves in the big wide ocean because their mother died to keep them alive. *The elephant mothers overcome this setback by sticking together, which this book will cover in a later chapter.*

The baby octopi swim around in the ocean with no supervision and no instruction, because there was no father there to assist in the parenting. These babies will grow up having to rely and survive off instinct, and we all know it is hard to survive off what you know if you don't know anything but what you know. You know? Life rarely gives its students a learning curve; either you know what you need to know or you die. *A child can only know what someone has taught them, what they have seen, or what they have figured out through experiential circumstances.* The life these teenagers are running around in is extremely difficult for them to figure out on their own.

Encourage some men to step up and be a role model in some boy's life, and quit putting the females in the position of sole provider, protector, and parent. Parenting is not a one-person job. For the women reading this book without a man at home you will have to take the role as the octopus or the bear mother. The bear mother provides for her cubs and sacrifices meals and her safety to ensure their survival.

By examining nature you can learn so much about parenting successfully in difficult environments. The giraffe parent teaches its child to run immediately after birth, and the same with the gazelle. They teach their kids early on in life how to avoid the pitfalls of life, and that is how we must be as parents. From the day your kids can comprehend, you should be preparing them for the life ahead of them. Teach your kids how to run. You do not give your kid the keys to the car until you or someone else has taught them to drive, right? Why would you give your kids the key to the city without first teaching them how to read the map?

It must start early on. Tell them more than "Do not talk to strangers" and "Do not stick metal inside the wall socket." These are very important things to teach them, but that is not the end of your parenting responsibility. You are not done once you have taught them not to drink Windex or play in the toilet.

Chapter Four

Six Barriers to Effective Listening and Six Tips for Effective Listening

Many people are difficult to talk to because no one ever taught them how to hold a conversation.

- Cederick W. Tardy II

The biggest challenge in our family was communication. Mark Twain once said, "If we are supposed to talk more than we listen, we would have two mouths and one ear." Humans were not created that way though. Most humans have two eyes, two ears, and one mouth. That means we should be watching and listening twice as much as we talk. *Silence at the opportune time allows opportunity for critical utterances to be heard and listened to.*

Anyone can talk, but it takes a dedicated person to listen. Listening does not occur as naturally as hearing. The two are different. I want to show you six barriers that hinder many people from listening effectively and six tips to enhance your ability to listen. The tips you are about to read are important for you to utilize as a parent because they enhance your ability to make meaningful conversation.

Hearing is only part of what listening actually is. Merely hearing something robs you of truth and understanding. Though the same member of the body makes use of both words, the ears, the difference in the two words lies in the definitions of listening and hearing.

Hearing is defined as perceiving sound "passively." Listening is defined as "actively" computing auditory information for the purpose of understanding and utilizing the information. The difference is in the "passiveness" involved in hearing, and the intense mental "activity" involved with listening. Listening is active. Hearing is letting the sound in one ear and right out the other without ever taking into consideration what was actually said.

As humans, we sometimes only "hear" things that do not strike a chord with our superficial wants. Those things that are not "meant for us," we deem as trash and let float past our ears. *The sad part is that all information is beneficial, and it is most often the case that the exact information you need in a difficult situation is*

15

Effective Listening

the exact information you disregarded at an earlier time. Many parents make this mistake and end up losing their children's trust and respect. Do not make this same mistake. The number one complaint of many kids is that no one listens to or understands them. Are they right?

Many parents only hear their kids, and they miss out on the opportune times to listen to their children's critical utterances. For example, a child is having a rough time fitting into a new neighborhood, and he is getting beat up every day. After a few weeks of not adjusting the child takes his own life. This is an extreme example of a parent who never listened to their child's complaints whether verbal or non-verbal (body language).

Hearing is what you do when you have heard a song too many times. It can be on as loud as the radio can go, you hear the beats and words, but they have lost all importance. You really are not listening to the song anymore. As a military police officer, I had to learn to listen and not just hear. When gathering information from a victim or suspect, I had to listen intensely, grasp all of the details, and then paraphrase the story so I could provide it in a statement. You, as a parent, might want to try similar tactics.

Below are six of the most common barriers to effective listening. I have defined a barrier as anything that impedes success or blocks the way of progress. Utilizing the lessons learned in this chapter will improve your ability to talk to your son.

One word of caution: The tips in this chapter are to improve daily, routine conversation, not for use when imposing guidelines or restrictions. If you try this stuff when laying down the law, your kids will run over you like a Mack truck!

Six Barriers to Effective Listening

1. *One barrier many cannot seem to overcome is the urge to read the mind of the person who they are speaking with.* These are people who try to guess what the other person is going to say next. Anyone who uses this "guess what's coming next tactic" is a poor listener because, instead of trying to listen to what is being said, they are finishing the story on their own. This type of person usually ends up with his or her own interpretation of the conversation.

Their feedback will be purely self-based and conceited. People who are always trying to guess what the other person is going to say next are impatient, selfish, and overconfident. This characteristic is devastating for parents because it robs the child of time to think clearly. This could be why your son is giving you the silent treatment. As a child it is sometimes hard to think of the right words to say. The mind of a child can hardly function under pressure. If you, as an adult, finish the sentence for your children, you rob them of thinking through their thoughts. In addition, you may even interrupt the child's train of thought and cause him to agree with your statement without truly meaning to or he may begin agreeing with your conclusion just to get the conversation over with faster and shut you up.

This only hurts you as the parent. You never get the true story. You only get what you wanted to hear and not what the child intended to say. As an effective listener, you will have to compel yourself not to finish a speaker's sentences.

2. *The second barrier that holds many people back is that they attempt to plan a rebuttal the entire time the other party is speaking.* The people who do this are not listening at all. They merely listen to one point, and then go straight into attack mode to figure out what they will say in response. Their mind is running so rampant that the rest of what was said has simply gone right over their heads. I believe my parents made this mistake, and I am guilty of doing this as well. Have you ever gotten into a verbal dispute with someone, but instead of listening to the other person, you spent your time thinking of how you will refute his or her points? Parents, this is why kids say that no one is listening to them. When they attempt to explain themselves to their parents, all they get in return is defensive rebuttals. After a few years of this treatment, any child will adopt the silent role. Hold back your rebuttals if at all possible.

3. *The third barrier occurs when people treat every conversation as a debate that they must win.* These people love to argue over everything. This "chronic-debater personality" will argue over whether to call a carbonated drink a soda, pop, coke, or soda pop.

This person considers every conversation as a debate. He or she might make an excellent lawyer or political figure, but they do a crappy job as a parent. Most kids do not like to argue or fight with their parents whether you believe me or not. Most kids just want to get their way or get on their way. Therefore, when you as a parent make every conversation a debate on whose beliefs are right or wrong, the child builds up resentment against you. It is hard to be an effective listener and a great debater.

The purpose of debating is to have a detailed argument already planned out in advance for the purpose of persuading the opponent. The debater is not interested in what the opposition has to say, because they already have their beliefs written out and they are going to stick with them. This is good for enforcing rules and regulations, but detrimental for holding a regular conversation. *You will never be an effective listener if you cannot learn to put your beliefs and values to the side while the other person speaks.* Debating is detrimental to the listening process.

4. The fourth barrier is by far the BIGGEST barrier to effective listening. Are you ready? *The biggest barrier made by a person in a conversation is believing that you are always right, have all the answers, and are smarter than the person talking to you.*

    If you let this barrier run your life, you will never be a good listener. Age, accreditation, occupation, education, or any other proviso that you may have over the other person does not mean you are any better then they are. You will fail as a listener every time you assume that you know it all or know more than the person you are talking to. You might run into someone who knows more than you one day and with a know-it-all attitude you will make a fool out of yourself.

    Additionally, you will fail as a listener every time you try to use your beliefs as the standard by which you judge someone else's beliefs. Just because you live your life one way does not make someone else queer or wrong for choosing to live his or her life another way, unless their way is legally, ethically, or morally wrong. Some form of legal system should be the standard on which beliefs are based, not your opinions.

    If your child likes crunchy bacon and you like chewy bacon, that does not make either one of you right or wrong, and since it is legal to eat chewy or crunchy bacon, then there really is no point in arguing over something so petty. Remember, these tips are for mundane conversations, not for setting rules and guidelines. Learn to understand and accept everyone's legally moral beliefs and you will become a more effective listener.

5. *The fifth barrier that blocks effective listening comes by asking too many questions at the wrong times in the conversation.* Questions are excellent for conversation, but an unprepared and ill-timed question will only confuse the speaker and interrupt their train of thought. People who interrupt a speaker with an out-of-place question at the wrong time are poor listeners. They are just as selfish as someone who attempts to finish the other person's sentences.

    How can you truly listen if you are interrupting with silly questions? For example: Your child is trying to tell you about what happened at school with his teacher or a bully, but every time he tries to finish a sentence, you ask him something like, "Well, why did you do that?" Too many questions asked at the wrong time hinder conversation.

    For a question to be valid in any conversation, it must only be asked when you are sure the other party has fully finished saying what they needed to say, and the question must be fully thought through. You need to know before you speak what and when you will say what you have to say. And remember that men respond better to specific, concise topics and questions.

6. *The sixth barrier is that many would be listeners simply fail to understand what the speaker is trying to say.* This may not be your fault at all, but it is detrimental for you as a listener. If you do not understand what was being stated, then you need to have a list of questions prepared, and you will need to ask them at the right time.

Remember, most people hate to repeat themselves and will consciously avoid people who they have to repeat themselves with continually. You will have to turn off the debate side of your brain, stop trying to think of what the person is trying to say and listen to what is really being said. No one, and especially a child, likes to speak with someone who does not understand what they are trying to say.

It is very frustrating to tell someone something and have them look at you with a blank expression. Do your best to quickly understand what your son is saying so he does not get fed up with you. If he is speaking too fast, ask him to slow down. Slang can be ambiguous and confusing. Ask for clarification. Ask him to repeat himself if he has lost you, but be sure to understand what is going on in the conversation.

Below are six tips to counter the six listening barriers. I have defined the word tip as any hint intended to promote success in any given process. Pay close attention, remain open-minded, and be sure to not only agree with what you read, but apply what you have read in your everyday life. One day you will need to teach your son these same things.

Six Tips for Effective Listening

1. Paraphrase: *The first tip to effective listening is making use of paraphrasing.* Paraphrasing means to recap what was said to you, in your own words. This is an effective way to enhance comprehension. When you are paraphrasing a statement, you are not asking a calculated question, but you are in some way questioning what you heard and expecting the speaker to correct any discrepancies.

With a conversational approach such as this, there is no possible way to mix up what the other person has said to you. Paraphrase what your children say to you to be sure you heard them correctly, understood correctly, and are on the same page. Be sure to avoid interrupting the speaker when paraphrasing.

Lastly, do not be afraid to take longer than normal pauses to gather your thoughts. What I mean is, when it is your turn to paraphrase, feel free to take as long as you need to gather your thoughts into a meaningful response. A mistake many people make is trying to speak without thinking thoroughly. When you are attempting to paraphrase someone's thoughts, you need to be sure you know exactly what you are going to say. Do not get uncomfortable; just take your time, as much time as you need, and then reply with an educated response.

2. Remain open-minded: *As an adult you will have to learn to remain open-minded to what is being said to you, especially to what your children say to you.* Do not get fired up because your child said something that may have rubbed you wrong, but instead, keep listening. Why? Because your child will soon learn what he can or cannot say to you.

A problem arises if you constantly attack your son for saying something outside of what's conventional, because a time will come when your son will need to tell you things that are out of the norm. Whenever you are going to need to know the truth in the future, he will assume that he cannot tell you because you will just get mad at him. As a result, he will hold the whole thing in, and leave you on the outside.

The end of this situation is that one day you will have a grown up child who you do not really know because you never gave him a chance to speak his mind freely. *Remain open-minded about what your child says to you, and as they grow to trust you more, they will confide in you more during those tough situations life will throw at them.* They will need someone to confide in, and that person will be the one who is willing to listen.

Recently, while hanging out with one of my relatives, I was shocked to hear her say that her friend's boyfriend's probation officer said "such and such" about him. My mind started racing. I wanted to cut her off and start refuting the fact that she has friends with boyfriends who are on probation at such a young age. And I wanted to make sure she understood that she should never have a boyfriend with a probation officer, but instead I held my tongue, calmed my nerves, picked right back up in the conversation, and held my thoughts until she was done.

Even after she was done I did not go right to the topic that was pressing on my mind, but instead I kept the previous conversation alive. Once it died, then I started my own conversation, not directly related to the pressing issue, but about boyfriends–good and bad ones. Chances are that next time she has something to say to me, she will not feel uncomfortable to tell me, because she knows that I am open-minded in my topics of conversation and willing to let her be the same. This example brings us to tip number three.

3. Hold your insights: *Hold your insights until the child is finished speaking and then at the right time add your point of view.* Here is a trick though: Instead of just stating your point of view, use a nudging technique, similar to what I did with my relative. I did not jump right on the boyfriends on probation issue, but instead nudged around the topic. The trick is to use perfectly timed and precisely planned questions to guide your children into your advice instead of trying to beat it into them.

   Instead of force feeding advice that you know is crucial for the development of your child, guide him slowly into it. The child will feel resentment, insufficient or inadequate if you are always giving them the right answers. If you can learn to use leading questions to make the child think through his situation until he reaches that "AH-HA" moment, it will make that advice stick better than if you just tell him. He will feel as though he thought of the solution all on his own, and as a result, build confidence in himself.

   Nudging Technique Scenario: Your child gets in a fight at school. You ask him what happened, get the story, paraphrase it, and then instead of telling him how he could have avoided it, you lead him into how he could have avoided it. Ask him, "What did you do wrong in that situation?" or "What could you have done better?" Slowly lead him to thinking through the situation. Let him learn. You just be the guide he needs.

4. Body Language: *Listening is not just an audible experience.* You can listen to the body language of an individual to truly grasp an understanding of what is going on. Someone's voice may give off an air of confidence, but the body language may show signs of sweating and twitching, which are signs of fear and a lack of self-confidence. Have you ever heard the expression, "Actions speak louder than words?" Is it true or not?

   It is crucial that you as a parent learn to listen to and "read" your child's body language. Trouble signs may not always be verbal, but there is always a clue as to what is going on in a child's head. Fidgeting, nervousness, paranoia and edginess are big signs that there is something seriously wrong. This is when you will need to use leading questions to pull out what is wrong. *Do not be fooled by confident words when the body language is saying otherwise.*

5. Place yourself in the other person's shoes: *While you are actively listening to what is being said, take the time out to reverse the roles.* Most people fail to make this simple change of thought when involved in a conversation. Imagine if whatever had happened to the other person had happened to you, and then ask

yourself how you would feel if the same thing had happened to you. In most cases, you cannot get mad at someone for what they have done if you put yourself in their shoes.

This does not go for things like theft, drugs, or murder, of course, but for things like a schoolyard fight, argument, and crying over something. You will be a more open-minded person if you can think about the conversation from the vantage point of the other person.

You do this by taking the time to intentionally think about what the other person may be feeling. Ask yourself, "Why are they saying and doing what they are doing?" Feel the air for cues as to how the other person feels. Put yourself in their shoes by saying, "What would I have done?" When you do this, you better prepare yourself to give advice or offer leading questions. It is only when you understand a person's circumstances that you can offer them accurate advice, so take the time out to see things from the other person's perspective.

6. Less talking is more: *As a listener, you are supposed to be listening. True listening does not involve talking at all.* If you are supposed to be listening, but you have taken control of the conversation, you have gotten off the path of what listening is.

Your job as a listener is to be a companion and a confidant, not a sparring partner. The less you speak when you are spoken to, the more people will come to you to speak; this is ideal if you want your kids to talk to you. When they are speaking, just shut up. Not to be rude in anyway, but just learn to hold back everything you want to say and just listen. They will love you for it. Remember, your body language is important as well. Just because you are not speaking, does not mean you can look off in the sky or do the dishes while your son is trying to speak to you. You will need to stop what you are doing and listen.

With all of these barriers and tips in mind, you are better prepared to take on the challenge of having a conversation with a teenager. If you follow these tips, and learn from these barriers, you will never hear, "You never listen to me!" ever again from your son.

This chapter may sound a little confusing. It may sound like I am contradicting myself when I say not to think about rebuttals while the other person is speaking, but then I say to think about what you are going to say next. Allow me to try my best to explain how the brain should be set to listen effectively. There is a certain amount of listening and thinking involved, but one should never outweigh the other. There is an exact measurement to be reached.

When truly listening, you should keep eye contact with an individual even if they are looking away. Listen to what is said, and then in your head repeat what they have just said to you. If the person is speaking too fast, then ask them politely to slow down so you can grasp what they are saying. As they are speaking, nonchalantly look them over a few times to judge their body language. All the while eagerly listen to them and make sure everything is registering in your brain.

Once they stop, and you feel you have a break to say something, pause for a moment to gather your thoughts, and then respond in a well thought-out manner with either a paraphrase or a leading question. This excites a response from the individual and they are usually more eager to keep speaking because they know that you are listening to them.

You should never be thinking of your response until the other person is fully finished speaking. Always feel free to take a few moments to register your thoughts before you reply. Do not automatically react, but instead respond. Respond in a respectful manner no matter what the age or education level of the person with whom you are speaking.

Constantly listen, register, and evaluate the individual from the top of the head to the soles of the feet. Here is something that I do when listening to others. I imagine what I would want from me if I were the one speaking, and then try to fulfill that unspoken request. I put myself in their shoes, but then go the extra step to correct or modify my behavior to fulfill the other party's expectations of a good listener. I imagine that this may sound like a lot of work, and it is certainly more work than the average person puts into a conversation, but we, as a people, need to stop trying to fit in with the average. The average parent produces an average kid.

Learn to listen and respond, and teach your kids to do the same. There is purposely not a section in the youth part of *The Connection Series* on the subject of listening. That is because I want you as parents to be able to teach your kids to listen by example and instruction. Additionally, I did not want to put these principles in the children's book because if they learn them faster then you do, they will resent you even more for not knowing how to listen to them!

In conclusion to what I hope was an informative chapter, I want to be sure that you wrote good notes from your own thoughts. If you feel that you have some excellent viewpoints to share, please feel free to send them to me *(cederick@ctardyenterprises.com* or by mail*)* for my own growth. *We are all learning. It would be foolish of me to think I know it all.* I know I need just as much help as everyone else in every area of life. We all have our weaknesses and issues, and if we take the time to help one another, this world will be a better place.

I recommend that you reread the six barriers and six tips from time to time to keep them fresh in your mind. Be sure to do your best to implement them into your life; it is up to you to teach your kids these principles. Your kids will listen to you better if they know how.

Remember: The number one complaint of most children is that no one listens to them or understands them.

Barriers to Effective Listening
1. Trying to be a mind reader while the other person is talking
2. Planning your rebuttal while the other person is talking
3. Attempting to turn every conversation into a debate
4. Believing that you are always right
5. Asking too many questions at the wrong times
6. Failure to understand what the speaker said

Tips for Effective Listening
1. Paraphrase what was said to you in order to understand what was said
2. Remain open-minded at all times
3. Hold your insights and hold your tongue until the person is done talking
4. Study the body language of the individual while they are speaking
5. Place yourself in the other person's shoes
6. Less talking is usually more

Chapter Five

Actions Speak Louder Than Words

If I were a parent, my number one continuous goal would be learning how to be a better father.
- Cederick W. Tardy II

Actions speak louder than words.

Many people hear the words above and pay them little mind. Many consider the phrase a simple, played-out cliché. But frankly, in my opinion, as a parent, one of the most prevalent thoughts in your mind should be, "actions speak louder than words." You should always remember this truism. Doing so will help you to decipher and understand more about your son's actions and behaviors.

This chapter is going to focus on two areas: body language and actions. *The body language and actions of an individual will say more about their character than the words they speak ever will.*

Body language is defined as the gestures, postures, and facial expressions by which a person manifests various physical, mental, or emotional states and communicates non-verbally with others. Actions refer to the things your son does, despite what he says. What I want is for mothers to gain an understanding of the gestures, actions, and facial expressions their child may make in order to determine what he is really thinking; not just what he is portraying.

Body Language: Communication through movements and mannerisms.
Actions: The actual behaviors of a human being.

Many experts believe that face-to-face communication is 55 to 90 percent body language, 7 to 25 percent choice of words, and 10 to 30 percent the way the words are said. *Body language and actions are well over 50 percent of communication.*

I know for a fact that for a parent, it is critical to gain knowledge of body language. Why? Simple. Over half of what your son is trying to tell you or not trying to tell you, he is saying nonverbally through his body language and actions. Learning how to read your son's nonverbal cues will give you added listening advantages. You will be much more adept at finding the truth or lies as your son is talking, and you will be able to make better parental decisions from there on out.

Let me explain where I learned the importance of body language. After I left naval boot camp, I was sent to a military police officer training school. There I first learned the importance of reading body language. I was not taught body language as a means of parenting, but as a tool and means of survival. I was taught to look for cues in the faces, hands, feet, shoulders, neck, and all over the body as signs of aggression or possible attack. The idea was that once I was aware of these signs, it would make me a better police officer. I would no longer have to wait until someone punched me in the face to react, but instead I could react to the nonverbal cues that indicated someone was about to act aggressively toward me.

I want for you to learn the importance of reading body language and actions so that you can react ahead of time, to prevent future mistakes your son may make. You will be able to recognize when your son is hurting, afraid, lying, being completely honest, and everything else, when you learn to read his body language and actions. For this reason I am passing down to you what I have learned.

The purpose of this chapter is to open your eyes to the 55 to 90 percent of nonverbal communication your boy is sending out that you may be oblivious to. Had my mother known these truths, she would have been much more capable of figuring me out before it was too late.

Preteens' and teenagers' biggest complaint is that no one, especially their own parents, understands or listens to them. On the other side, parents complain that their kids are not talking to them, which also could be considered a true statement. Well, maybe? The kids are in fact talking to their parents, just not in words. The youths are speaking more through their body language and actions. Many parents have just been blind and deaf to this fact.

Below is how a fictitious incident may go between a single mother and her son. Imagine your own typical episodes with your son as I paint this picture. At the end we will see just how much more there is to this story when we consider the body language and actions of the boy, rather than just his words.

The boy walks into his house at around 5:30 in the afternoon, on a school day, where he got in trouble that day, but is not sure his mother knows about it yet. As he walks in the front door, he slowly and quietly closes it. His mom is in the kitchen.

Not wanting to be noticed, the boy quickly cuts a right turn around the corner, makes a B-line to his room and closes the door. The mother, being the good mother she is, walks into the boy's room, which startles him.

She looks in and notices that the boy seems a little shaken up. His mom asks him, "How was your day at school?" With his hands in his pockets, looking down and around at the floor to avoid eye contact, he replies, "Fine." As his mother continues to talk to him, he begins to get restless and fidgets a little. He sighs with his hands now crossed over his chest. His mother senses that he may be tired. He tells her he has a project from school to work on with his friend who lives around the corner, so he is going to go over to his house to work on it. She says, "Be back before 9:00 tonight," and goes back into the kitchen wondering why her son will not talk to her.

As fictitious as this was, it is not too farfetched from how many families live their lives. Allow me to elaborate on what could actually be going on if we study body language and actions.

If I were the parent, I would be sure to know that school ended at 2:30 in the afternoon. I would be suspicious as to why my son is home so late (studying actions), and why he did not just go straight to his friend's house if he had to work on a school project (studying actions). As I said in the story, the boy got in trouble at school. He had to stay after for detention, and his mother never knew about it. She should have asked a question. If the boy never closes the front door quietly, for him to do it this time means he probably has something to hide, and the fact he went straight to his room would add to that suspicion (studying actions).

If it startles your son when you walk into his room, he is probably doing something wrong, but not necessarily! He could just be jumpy, but most likely he is doing something wrong. If he were just watching TV or playing video games, he would just glance over at you, but when he is doing something wrong and someone pops in it will startle him. As a mother you would want to know why he is acting nervous (studying body language). But you don't just flat out ask him. Use leading questions to get some answers.

Hands in the pockets generally means he had something in his hands when he was startled and tried to put it in his pockets, or it means he is nervous in general (studying body language).

Whenever anyone avoids eye contact, it generally means they are lying, have something to hide, are disgusted with the person they are talking to, or some other negative thing (studying body language). The clues he was displaying should have alerted the mother to be more concerned as to what was REALLY going on with her son that day. She asked the general question, "How was your day?" *But remember, when asking someone, especially a guy a question, it needs to be one that cannot be answered with a simple one-word answer if your intent is to strike up a conversation.* His one-word answer is natural then, because the opportunity was there.

As the boy fidgets, the mother should be wondering, "Why the heck is he still acting so nervous well after I startled him, and why are his hands still in his pockets?" (studying actions and body language) Sighs and quick answers show that the person is agitated, which usually means they are ready to get out of the conversation before it turns ugly. Arms crossed over the chest is a sign of defense, like guarding the heart.

As I stated earlier, the mother should be wondering why her son did not start on his project earlier, and ask him why he is not starting until so late in the afternoon. *His story will generally come out jumbled, if he does not already have something prepared.* Keep nudging at him to search for the truth. When you do let him go to so-and-so's house, do not just let him go without calling the person, asking them what they are going to do, and ask to talk to the parents. Be proactive, it's the only way.

Can you see how much more detailed the incident became once you began to look at the nonverbal cues? It can go even deeper mothers. The more signs you are able to pick up, the better you will be as a protective mother. My mom could have done a better job at reading my nonverbal cues. She could have been a lot more proactive. She could have stopped a whole lot of things before they happened.

You do not have to interrogate your son as a cop would interrogate a suspect. All you have to do is ask more questions, and make sure the questions take more than one word to answer. Also, be a bit subtle when you investigate. Do not kick down his front door because your son will just run out the back. Knock on the door instead (ask rational questions) and he will answer the door. If you have questions about his behavior because of the cues you have noticed, always inquire about them. Do not let yourself be fooled any longer.

As a military police officer, I was trained to look for all of the following cues:

Facial expressions – Though easy for some experienced con-artists to manipulate, facial expressions are hard to control. Things such as scrunching of the forehead, squinting of the eyes, frowning, smiling, or wiggling the nose happen without much conscious effort. They are things to be mindful of, because they say so much.

Eye quivers – Actual eyeball movement. Most people are not able to control their eyeballs when they are nervous, lying, or scared. Their eyes will flutter out of control, or constantly be moving. A calm person will look straight ahead. For a person to look up and to the right when answering questions is normal. However, when they break their norm and look up and to the left or down, they are most likely lying to you at that point.

Posture – Slouching generally means low self-esteem. A straight back generally means high self-esteem. Slouching also is a sign of laziness.

The walk – A person who walks fast has a purpose that they are eager to get back to. If your boy walks as if he has a limp, he may be trying to be a thug. Hanging the head down while walking is a sign of low self-esteem. Does he walk with both hands in his pockets?

The talk – Everyone talks differently. You can pick up a lot of things just by how a person talks without even listening to what they have to say. Consider the following:
  a. Whether they use slang – Slang terms can tell you where a person is getting their influences from. But, you have to know where the slang comes from. Do your research. If the source is music then find out the artists. If it is a friend then find out which friend. When you know whether the slang or lingo comes from rap, rock, rhythm and blues, movies, gangs, drug talk, friends, and the like you will know what influences him.
  b. The speed a person talks – Nervous people talk fast. Calm people talk at a normal tempo. Scared people talk fast. Arrogant people enunciate every single syllable. People with low self-esteem mumble.
  c. Volume of speech – People with low self-esteem will talk so low that you can barely hear them. Pompous folks talk loudly so everyone will notice them. Agitated people talk loudly, but really upset people may mumble or talk through their teeth so you can barely hear them.
  d. Vocabulary – Same as slang. Word usage tells you exactly what a person is thinking. You can also tell whether someone is educating himself or not by the words they use in their normal speech. You can tell a person's influences by their vernacular. Many gangs have key words they use that let you know which group they are affiliated with.

Hand and feet movements – Rubbing the nose, pacing, swinging hands back and forth, and cracking knuckles are all signs of aggressive behavior or nervousness. Talking with the hands generally denotes excitement.

Hairstyle – Many people have the same haircuts, but if your son is going through a crazy phase, spiked hair, or something off the wall, he is getting into rock and roll and stuff like that. Do your research to find the source of the influence.

Body markings – Scars and tattoos – Scars all over the head, face, and body tell the tale of a combatant. Tattoos, depending on what they are and where they are, can be gang related, but often they are just an expression of the self. Every tattoo tells a story so be sure to ask.

General demeanor – Find out exactly how your son acts when he is in a normal state of mind, and then base every other behavior of his off of his normal behavior. *From this you can determine what settings make him uncomfortable or what environments he thrives in.*

Jewelry – Lots and lots of gold, silver and platinum jewelry are stereotypical for drug dealers and pimps, or wannabe's. Leather watches generally indicate relaxed and casual. Silver generally says, "I want to be seen."

Hygiene – Dirty boys with no respect for their appearance may have some self-esteem issues. A clean-cut boy who is always worried about his appearance may be a little lady's man. Manicures and waxing do not necessarily connote homosexuality.

Clothes – Style of dress tells a lot about a person. You can tell whether someone is very casual in their demeanor, suited for business, or into sports by their clothes. Shirts with writing or pictures on them say what the wearer wants to be known and recognized by.

Music – *For youths, music often says what we would like to say to the world. (Read that over twice.) The music your son listens to is saying aloud things he says or he wishes he could say aloud.*

Posters on the walls – These show his idols and the things he wishes he was or had.

As a military police officer, I would evaluate everything I could think of to determine what a person was really saying, despite what they were telling me. People lie. It is important to pick up on body language cues because they will often say what your son may be trying to cover up with his words. Body language will often contradict his words if he is lying. Body language expresses the truest emotions, feelings, and attitudes. I recommend you believe what his body language and his actions are saying over what his mouth is saying. Subconscious thoughts and body language are beyond his level of control, but his words are easy for him to manipulate. Don't be fooled.

The best thing for parents to do is find out how their son acts at school; one of his normal settings. If you have to have covert e-mail correspondence with your son's teachers on a regular basis, then do so. Chances are your son's teacher knows things about him that you would never have dreamed could be true, positively or negatively.

If you are oblivious to reading your son's actions and believe everything he says, then you will be gamed. Gamed means toyed with, played with, fooled, bamboozled, hoodwinked, got! If he says he is going to do "A," but his actions, or the result of his actions, show that he is not doing "A," do not believe he is doing "A." For example: Your son says he is going to go to school every day and do better to keep his grades up, but day after day he comes home and watches TV, never does any homework, and says he did it all at school. Do not believe him. Call his teacher to find out how his actions are at school, and then assess him by those actions.

Another example: I used to tell my mother I was not doing drugs anymore. My words said that I was clean, but my actions and results told the real truth. I was still hanging out late, even on weekdays. I still came home reeking of smoke, which I would say came from the pool house. (As if I really went there every day.) I still had violent mood swings. I was still lazy. I was still spending all of my money with nothing to show for it. I was still behaving the same in every way. In this case, it was clear by my actions I had not changed anything, and a surprise urine test would have shown that to be true.

Always judge a tree by its fruit, and always judge your son by his fruit, namely, the results.

I have gotten so good at reading body language and actions, that I can sometimes tell what a person's favorite TV shows are just by how they act. I can see the influence the shows have on their personality that is.

Parents think their kids do not talk to them, but that is not true. The communication is just nonverbal. Your kids are crying to you, but you have to learn to listen with your eyes and not just your ears.

Your kids are crying out in their music. If all the music they are listening to is talking about sex, drugs, or shooting, then that is what they are into. They will try to emulate those things, so be on the lookout for whatever you hear from their music. Take the time to listen attentively to what they are listening to. By doing this you will hear what they want to say, or what they are saying when they are not around you.

Your kids are crying out in their fashion. Your kids are crying out in their activities. Your kids are crying out in their favorite movies. Had my mom known my favorite movie was *Half Baked* she would have had a clue that I was a pothead. Your kids are crying out in their circle of friends. Look at what their friends are doing. Birds of a feather really do flock together. Your kids are crying out in their classes at school and their grades. When I was at school I was completely different than who I was at home. I recommend having parent-teacher conferences regularly, even if your son is in high school, for insight into your son's actions. Find out who he hangs around with at school. Find out the types of disrespectful things he may say at school. You may find out your son is a good kid. Your kids are crying out in their favorite foods, their favorite books, if they read at all, and their lifestyle in general. Do not try to be a military police officer. Be more attentive to nonverbal cues. Be a proactive parent first. Then try to be a friend.

Chapter Six

Avoid Discouragement

Sometimes hope is all you have to cling to, but it is better then nothing at all. Lose your hope and what do you have?

- Cederick W. Tardy II

I believe that if you lose your hope for better, your son will lose his hope for better. The rest of this chapter is based on this premise.

I have come to notice that whenever someone fails at anything, there is always one common ingredient: The person's failure occurred at the peak of discouragement–when things got really hard. I believe that the greatest cause of failure is discouragement. Examine your own life for moments that you've failed. Was there some point in time when the circumstances became exceedingly unbearable and you became dispirited? As yeast is the active ingredient in baking that makes dough rise, discouragement is the active ingredient that causes failure to rise.

Some may argue that failure is caused by inadequate knowledge, skill, or training, but there are many who succeed without the proper skills, talent, training, or knowledge. These people know that as long as you remain open-minded and optimistic, your mind will work out a solution to solve the problem. When there is a will, the willing will find a way.

I believe that to avoid discouragement you must do two things. First, focus on encouraging yourself, because your attitude determines your altitude and your son's altitude. Feed yourself positive thoughts when you are up, and devour a smorgasbord of positive thoughts when you are down. Elevate yourself single mother, because no one else will.

Second, I believe you should get help and advice from others. A great start would be a long-time, trusted friend. If this person is a successful parent, then I suggest you ask them what they are doing right, and what you are doing wrong. Be as open as you can with this trusted person, and genuinely listen to their advice.

If you seek advice from a person who is not a parent at all, make sure they are positive, successful, and not gossipers, and then tell them enough about the situation for them to get a good picture of what is going on. Maybe they can give you some helpful insight from their own youthful experiences.

Avoid Discouragement

When you are asking for advice, make sure you give off an air of confidence, as if you are just asking for an opinion, not begging for a solution. *The vibe that you give off when talking to someone will subconsciously affect their receptors and that will affect the type of advice they give you.* If you come to them in a needy manner, they will give you some sappy, hang-in-there type of advice, but if you ask them with a true heart and confidently, you are more likely to get a truthful answer that will be pertinent to help your situation.

No matter what happens, you should always remain optimistic and open-minded. Remain open-minded to the responses you may get. Some may hurt, and others may not be applicable, but do not disregard anyone or any type of wisdom because it may not fit for you at that time. You may need it later down the line.

As you are taking in the advice, remember that you are not the same person as they are. You have a different temperament, and so their parenting style will not always match with yours. That is okay, as long as you remember not to compare your parenting style to theirs. Additionally, remember not to compare your children with someone else's children. Yes, it would be nice to have great children like someone else, but comparing the two is not going to help your kid any. Unfair comparisons are a recipe for disaster.

When gathering this outside advice, your objective is not to compare, but to glean. Gleaning means taking or gathering. Your job is to gather all of the pertinent wisdom you can, like a sponge, and only use what works for you. If you have used a sponge before then this next parallel will make a lot of sense. When you grab a sponge, it is soaked full of soapy water, but you do not need all of that soapy water, so you wring it out and use the remainder to clean the area you intended to. You should do the same with wisdom given to you by multiple sources. Take all the advice you can get, wring out what you do not need, and clean up your situation with what works. This is what my mom did.

Now that her hardest moments as a parent are over, my mother credits a lot of her strength in the midst of the fight to her true friends who were able to give her encouragement during the hard times. Times she was crying all night, for days on end. She constantly says that if it was not for good friends giving her wisdom, hope, and encouragement, she most likely would have given up on me.

Here is something else to consider. Without hope and courage, your imagination will fade away. Imaginations are not just for kids. You need your imagination to keep up with your kid. You need to imagine things like what you would be doing to get into trouble at his age and in his position. When you can imagine those types of things, you can set up roadblocks in advance to protect your son from traveling a dead-end road. Your imagination is your best asset. Imagination feeds off zeal.

As you work to avoid discouragement, stay focused on the future and not the present. Even if your child may be drinking, smoking, and acting a complete fool right now, his life is not over yet. You must learn to envision the "not over yet" part of his life while you are making steps to get him turned around.

Here are a few how-to steps to envision a better day: The first step is gaining an understanding of what you want or need to do. It makes so much sense and is so simple that it can almost be confusing. If you do not know where you want your kid to end up, how will he end up there?

The second step is to implant that vision into your brain. You do this by whatever means you choose. Personally, I like confession statements, reading literature specific to my vision, drawing pictures, meditating, or repetitiously talking about what I want as ways to implant a vision into my mind. Whichever way your brain computes information the best, use that means.

The third step is making a plan to get your son to the place you envisioned for him. Make sure that the set place you have envisioned for him is a reasonable destination, and then build a reasonable plan to get him to that destination.

Lastly, work the plan. (Consult the chapter on planning.)

I recommend having checkpoints or markers in the plan that measure success. Checkpoints put a goal that looks huge into bite-sized morsels. The purpose of these points is to visually encourage you to get to the next one. These points are where you can stop for a brief moment and pat yourself on the back for accomplishing them. It is crucial for your self-esteem and hopefulness that you encourage yourself as a single mother. Appreciate every small victory as if it were the final victory. As a single mother, there is really no one there to appreciate you but yourself, so take advantage of that fact.

It is nearly impossible to become discouraged when you have a vision in your mind, a plan in your hands, and are seeing success at every mile marker. There is no room to become discouraged when you have drive and focus. If you have a go-getter's attitude you will have a go-getter's altitude.

You may be thinking: "But Cederick, how long will it take for my son to change his ways? I just cannot take it anymore!"

Answer: The amount of effort that you put into your child's development will probably return half the results of that effort. What I mean is, if you put in 100 percent effort, you will likely see a 50 percent difference in your child's development. These results are not the product of one day's work, but of effort purposely expended over a substantial period of time.

I am an investor and I know from an investor's point of view, putting in 100 percent to only get half of that back looks like a poor choice of investment. If we were talking stocks or real estate, then I would not recommend these returns, but we are talking about your son's life. Any amount of return in your child's life is

Avoid Discouragement

worth the investment.

So what do you do if you want to see a 100 percent turn around? *Do your very best to give 200 percent effort every day for a substantial period of time.* To get a full turn around from your son is going to take two times your full effort. Additionally, 200 percent does not mean that you should do twice as much as you are doing now, because right now you may not be giving 100 percent. One hundred percent means working at your maximum potential as a parent. That means you are the Magnum P.I. of the parenting world. You are into everything and know everything about your child. You have plans and routes set up for his success. And you are avidly involved in his becoming a successful adult. That is what it takes to give 100 percent as a parent. The average parent doesn't do all of that.

Doubling their present effort will not produce the 200 percent effort needed to produce the 100 percent turnaround. But it will get at least get them to where they should have been initially. This is not an attack on you mothers. This is reality. Sorry parents have become so prevalent that the government has had to step in and take action. Things are out of control when Uncle Sam has to play stepfather.

If 100 percent means that you have to be Magnum P.I., then 200 percent means that you have to be Sherlock Holmes and MacGyver all rolled into one. You have to have twice the imaginative potential, twice the drive to study, investigate, plan, and research. What are you thinking about right now? Write it down.

Don't shoot for the 200 percent off the bat though. Set a reasonable goal first to get to the 100 percent level, and then when you are ready, double all of your efforts. Do this and you will speed up the progression of the "teenage boy to man transformation." All of this is possible. The parents who put this amount of effort into their child's development are not the ones who have problems with their kids when they become adults. By age 22 to 23 their kids have graduated college and gone on to pursue a career or business endeavor. At 30 or 40, they start a family. There are no Western Union funds transfers or collect calls from jail for these fully engaged parents.

It took me years to finally grow up and think straight. If your son is a Loony Toon, you cannot expect him to straighten out in six months. An easy way to discourage yourself is to set a goal that you cannot achieve. You cannot get discouraged and lose hope if after six months, a year, or more, you still see little or no change. Remember to be reasonable.

In conclusion, bear in mind that your spirit has to stay resolute in order to turn your child's life around. Discouragement is the active ingredient in failure, just as yeast is the active ingredient in baking.

Know in your heart and mind that you can and will overcome as long as you have a vision in your heart and a plan in your hands.

- Cederick W. Tardy II

Chapter Seven

Taking the Reigns and Being the Leader as a Mother

A leader is like the lookout of a maritime vessel, a visionary. Leaders consider the big picture and survey the circumstances. When they see danger or opportunity, they beckon with a loud call, "Veer right!" or "Land straight ahead!" A leader is a farsighted visionary.

- Cederick W. Tardy II

Human relations is the most critical component of becoming a great leader. It is said that leading a human being is a lot like pushing a piece of string, but have you ever tried to push a piece of string? It is difficult at best. What tends to happen is the end you are pushing coils up. It is nearly impossible to push a string just as it is nearly impossible to lead, push, or force a human, no matter their age, to go against their will. Instead of trying to push string, common sense says that you should pull on it to get it to go in the direction you intend for it to go. That suggests leading from the front.

This same logic applies to humans, and yes, even to your son. His whole life you might have been trying to push him around. That would explain why he folds up and refuses to go in your intended direction. Next time, pull him in the direction you intend for him to go. Lead from the front. Show him it is alright to take that oh so scary first step.

Lead your son by example. Pull him with an eagerness to understand his point of view. Pull him into your viewpoint with calculated statements. Pull your son with empathetic questioning. *The best leaders do not push their followers into jeopardy, but step out in front of their followers and show them that the ground ahead is safe to tread.*

Random Advice: The mother who is disrespected by her child has not shown her child that she is the parent–the ruler of the household.

Most times a frustrated mother, after working a job or two or three, comes home and the last thing she wants to hear is a disobedient smart-aleck comment.

Taking the Reigns

But, just as you wish for your son to understand your viewpoint, you must understand his. I know this sounds ridiculous, but believe me, you need to obtain both sides of the problem before you can come to an understanding or solution.

Take the time to evaluate and not just stipulate. Often after evaluating the cause of the disobedience you will find that both sides of the arguments, yours and your son's, are valid and often quite similar. There may be a couple of minor disagreements, but for the most part, you will agree on everything that is considered a problem. This is where you will need to learn to pull on him and not push him into submission. A man offended is harder to win over than a strong city.

A leader must understand the mind of her followers. Single mothers, must understand the mind of their son. You must not underestimate the value of talking to your child and inquiring into his outlook, however simple it may seem. You cannot go around kicking, screaming, and throwing fits to get your son to listen to you, to pay attention, and to respect you. He will just think you are a crazy woman. How mad would you get if he acted this way towards you? Why then would or should his reaction be any different from yours? A strong leader is one who is respected by their followers. A strong leader is one who is trusted to lead their followers to success. Does your son respect, trust, and believe in you enough to follow you, or follow your orders?

Have you exerted yourself as the one in command? This might be the reason he never does what you tell him to do. Let me try to wrap this in a story. This story has nothing to do with parenting; it is about following an incompetent leader. In this story, I explain the thoughts of a youth when he is given an order, from a leader he does not trust. This is a true story to the best of my recollection. I recommend you take the story as a whole, and at the end attempt to apply it to your situation.

In my first year in the Navy, I was sent to a tactical ship boarding training school where I participated in a training environment similar to a game of paintball, a game where guns are fitted to shoot balls of paint instead of lead bullets. The paintballs are shot by compressed air instead of gunpowder, and the game is considered fun. When the paintballs make impact they do hurt and leave a bruise, but it is all in the fun of the game.

The school was set up to teach us strategic ship boarding and threat elimination onboard a naval vessel. There was one particular training scenario that forced my would-be S.W.A.T. team down a narrow passageway and out into an open area in the middle of the ship. In this open area there was a sniper that we could hardly see shooting down on us with no remorse. I, being the kind of person I am, ducked and hid behind a wall. I did not want to get shot. Can you blame me? If it had been real life, I would have ducked for cover. Wouldn't you?

This sniper, in less then five seconds, shot two of my team members. I was the third person in a line of seven, but since the two people in front of me just died, I was now first in line. Instead of being shot, I decided to take cover and think of a plan. However, I was not the leader and could not make plans for the team. Instead, the team leader had to make the plans.

What was his bright plan? He decided that it would be a smart idea to send a person, me, to stand in the same exact spot where the other two people had just been shot, thinking if I stood there, I could provide cover fire for us to get through the open area.

Imagine this for a second. You are holding guns, people are shooting at you, two people are dead in front of you, and the lead person in your team says go stand over there where those two people were just shot. Crazy or what?

Well as you can guess, I told the leader he could shove that idea. I was not going to go stand in that spot.

We argued on the wall in that passageway for a few seconds. Instead of sending me, he sent another person over to that spot of death. All I can say is "rest in peace." He was shot before he even got there. So now there were three people dead out of a team of seven. This sniper was eating our team alive, and we could not go back the other way. It was down to our last four people. The other two, the two besides the leader, believed in what I was saying and they all decided not to go stand where the leader was directing them. Even though there were three dead people on the ground, the leader decided to go over to that spot anyway. May he rest in peace as well; he did not make it very far before catching a few rounds.

You may be asking, "What is the moral of this story?" Well, here it is. The leader of my team, even though he was a higher rank than I or anyone else on the team, just like you are higher ranking than your son in the household, got no respect because he had a *poor track record*. I did not have to take an order from him to know he was incompetent. All I had to do was look and see the dead people he had just led. A good leader is trusted, but a bad leader sends his men into a barrage of bullets.

Your son is looking at you in much the same way. He will not listen to what you order him to do if you have a bad track record. If you have ever told him that you were going to do something and you did not come through, that is just like each one of those dead bodies on the ground. Every parental mistake you have made is just like one of those dead bodies. It only took two dead bodies for me to realize the guy was a poor leader. *How many casualties do you have on your record?*

It only took my mom a few times to mess up her trust with me before I concluded she did not know what she was doing. Whether I was right in my assumption or not, I began disregarding her orders. In short, I began giving her a hard time and questioning everything she had to say, just as I questioned the team leader's judgment in the story.

Her credibility had been shot down. Her track record was outlined in chalk as far as I was concerned. The good thing about trust is that it can be resurrected. Amen! Trust can be brought back to life. My trust in my mother's words had been dead for years, but after she began to make many significant positive changes in her life, she brought her accountability back to life. Instead of making promises she could not keep, she would just say no. I respected her more for the "no." I, and most people in this world, would rather hear no than yes, make plans for the yes, and then find out instead it was really a no. You know?

Lying or making promises you cannot keep is the quickest way to raise a disobedient child. In many cases, disobedience from a child stems from the unreliability of the parent's behavior. If the child does not see the parent doing what is right, he will become conditioned to believe he doesn't have to either. After all, mom isn't doing what is right. If you are going to be the leader, you will have to be a good leader. A good leader has a good track record.

A good leader does not lead by barking orders, but by setting the example. A good leader of a child is always doing her best to be the perfect example. *The model of excellence should be your goal with every breath you take.* Remember that your child is watching you, just as you watched your parents. You may not remember everything your parents did, but I guarantee that your actions and beliefs are a result of their behaviors. The same rule will apply to your child. He may not remember everything that you did when he is older, but he will be affected by your behaviors, positively or negatively. Make your affect on him positively effective.

A good leader will not continue to make the same mistakes repeatedly. The leader in my training scenario kept making the same mistakes time after time, and that is why I concluded he was incompetent. I understand that everyone cannot always think clearly under pressure, but *at least have enough clarity of mind to ask for help when you cannot see a way out.*

If you are constantly making the same mistakes, expect some mouthing off from your son just as I mouthed off to the leader. It is not right, and I am not saying you have to take it, but just expect it. I cared more about my safety and my wellbeing than that man's orders. Those men would have been killed in real life had that person really been a team leader.

If you are constantly showing yourself to be unfit for the parenting role because you are under too much pressure, then please, ask for help! Stop taking bullets. Stop breaking promises and destroying your credibility. Stop doing anything that does not lead to success. Ask for help from anyone you know who can point you in the right direction. If you are heading in the right direction, then your son, who is following you, will be heading in the right direction.

Like pulling a string, you hold on tight, chart a path, and step out first as the leader. The string has no choice but to follow your finger when you lead this way. But, if you push that string from behind, you will both get nowhere.

Chapter Eight

Rebuilding Lost Trust

Before anyone else can trust you, you have to be able to trust yourself.
— Cederick W. Tardy II

This chapter is written to the mother who wonders what she did that was so wrong, and honestly has no clue that she has messed up horribly. In order to be the best parent for your son you will need to have his trust, plain and simple. *Without his trust, all of your years of instruction, wisdom, and guidance will fall on deaf ears.*

Often it is not the children who lose the trust of their parents first, but the other way around. Typically, the child loses faith in his father or mother long before he is old enough to make mistakes big enough to rob the faith of his parent. The reason is that a child sees his mother and father as idols or super heroes–super heroes who are not allowed to make mistakes.

When a parent makes mistakes it hurts the child more than most parents realize. When a single mother, busy and tired from a long day at work, forgets to pick her son up from daycare or football practice, it kills him inside. The pain of an incident like this has the effect of a seismic jolt along the fault line of the heart. It tears him apart, and he begins to wonder what happened to his super hero. It is as if all of a sudden the woman who he cried out to for help all his life is not there for him any more. He starts to doubt, he starts to lose his faith, and he starts to lose his trust.

Knowledge, wisdom, and sound guidance cannot pass through the barrier of mistrust. Trust is crucial in the mother-and-son relationship. Without a high level of trust, you are asking for rebellion. Your kid will not believe in what you tell him because you have neglected him a few too many times. You will never be able to get through to him. Everything you say will fall on deaf ears, on ears of bitterness.

Imagine your son as a city and you are his neighboring city. When a neighboring city cannot trust the city next to it, it prepares for war! It builds a tall and strong barrier, barricade, or defensive structure. In the same way, your son will begin building a partition at the exact moment he realizes he cannot trust you. His defenses will be strong, and his barrier will seem impenetrable. *His defenses are strong because the problem now involves his pride and his emotions, two things he knows little about managing.*

As you know, your son is extremely impressionable. Everything you are doing now is molding his personality. Everything said or done at this stage in his life has dramatic influence on who he is and who he will grow to be. His mind, personality, and temperament are in the making.

There are numerous things that can cause a child to lose faith in his mother, but I have to say that the number one cause of faith loss is promises that have repeatedly not been upheld. "I will do that tomorrow," you tell your son, but tomorrow comes without your adherence to your word. Tomorrows come and go, but YOU never come through. You believe in your heart, "He is just a child; he will get over it," which is true. It is true; your son will get over it, but how he will get over it is the question.

Will he get over it by running away, by years of rebellion, or through drug abuse? How will he get over it?

As I said, there are numerous causes to a child losing faith in their parents. Drug abuse and addiction, addiction to gambling, sexual recklessness, alcoholism, physical abuse, verbal abuse, poor financial decisions, poor economic decisions, and the list goes on and on. The point is that there are more ways for a parent to lose the faith of their child than for the child to lose the faith of their parent. You hold the responsibility. You are the adult, the super hero. He is just a kid, nothing more, and nothing less.

Below, I have listed 15 suggestions for you to use in conjunction with one another in hopes of rebuilding lost trust. You will have to let your pride as a parent pass away for now and work on building the bridge over his moat. *You will have to lose the attitude of, "He is the kid and I am the parent," because you are the example and he is the impressionable young mind.* His life is in your hands. Take these suggestions to heart. Feel free to tweak and work them as you see fit, but do not feel free to drop those you do not agree with, because you may indeed drop them all depending on your level of stubbornness.

If you are prepared to reestablish the lost trust between you and your son, and tear down his protective fortifications so that what you say to him can actually get through, you must be willing to apply the pointers below:

1. The first thing that you must do as a parent is *admit that you have made mistakes.* Admitting that you have failed in some area is the first step. Once you realize that you have messed up, you will be more willing to change the faults you have, instead of overlooking them in hopes of changing some outside factors, many of which cannot be changed.

2. Second, you must *forgive yourself for your mistakes*. After you have taken the blame for your wrongdoings, and decided to no longer hide behind a wall of excuses, you must make a decision to forgive yourself for your mistakes. It is hard to be hit with the reality that you may be flawed as a mother, but there is no such thing as the perfect mother. If you hold yourself prisoner to your mistakes, you will have no energy or will to make any changes to correct them.

3. The next thing you should do is *sincerely apologize to your son*. Just say, "Son, I am sorry for..." Whatever the case or cases may be. Fill in the blank as appropriate.

4. After you have forgiven yourself and apologized, you must be woman enough to confront your son honestly, and *request that he forgive you for your mistakes*. Let him know that you are not a perfect mother, but you are willing to make some changes to heal his hurt. Let him know that you want his trust. Let him know that you know you have messed up, but you are going to put in a dedicated effort to transform. Let him know some of the fears you have of being a mother in a way that he can understand what you are saying.

5. *Avoid the guilt trips* that he may try to place on you, or that you may try to place on yourself. I used to tell my mother that it was too late for her to start being a mother. She had to ignore these statements. You cannot change the past at all. Let your guilt go, and if your son tries to hold you up and blame you for your past, stop him cold in his tracks. You are no longer who you were if you have decided it is in your best interest to change. However, you have no right to stop him if you have not made an effort to change for the better.

6. I recommend, if you are truly serious, that you *ask your son to help keep you in check*. Be willing to respect him when he questions your actions. Your son will be more honest with you than you will be with yourself. Adhere to his suggestions. It will be humbling, but what's wrong with humility?

7. *Set yourself a punishment* for lying or breaking your son's trust. Do not try to believe that you will never make a mistake again, because you will. We all make mistakes. Concentrate on trying to minimize the number of mistakes you make. You are trying to be a better mother, not a "like all the rest mother." Your punishments should be whatever you deem worthy enough for the occasion.

8. *Ask your child for his suggestions or advice* to make you a better parent. His personal suggestions will benefit you and make you a better parent, for him. He will be honest with you. This avenue of communication will add more insight than I ever could, because it will be specialized instruction directly from your son to you.

9. *Develop a proven track record of unbroken promises.* You can talk righteous until you are blue in the face, but if there are no actions, no results, it is all in vain and good for nothing. Your son will only gain trust in you when he has seen evidence to prove you are trustworthy. Be consistent when overcoming your shortcomings.

10. *Stop making promises that you cannot keep.* Do not promise to get your son golf clubs, a puppy, or a car if you cannot afford one. Do not say you are going to take him to Disneyland at the end of the year if you know it may not be a sure thing. Only make promises that you can keep. Your son will hold you liable to everything you say you will do, just like a creditor.

11. *Follow through with your personal commitments to yourself.* Many people make the mistake of saying they are going to do something, but then they never do it. Do you know anyone who is always saying they are going to go to school, get a better job, or be faithful? Every time they tell you they are going to do something, you just roll your eyes and say, "Yeah right!" This is exactly what your son is thinking if you are not sticking with your personal goals and promises.

12. *Live by the definition of honor.* Honor is principled uprightness of character and personal integrity.

13. *Surround yourself with good friends*, and only bring home men and women who are good influences and examples for your son to see you around. If you have to hide someone from your son because he or she drinks, cusses, abuses you, or uses you, then maybe you should really be hiding that person from yourself. The people your son sees you around will impress a picture of who you are in his mind.

14. *Be patient.* This is one of the premier things you can do. Be patient with yourself. Recognize that rebuilding lost trust will be difficult, time consuming, embarrassing at times, but in the end, well worth the struggle!

15. *Do not be afraid to seek professional assistance.* Maybe a sexual, alcoholic, narcotic, gambling, or some other addiction is too hard for you to break alone. For this reason, we have people specially trained to help you. Do not feel ashamed to seek help, religious or secular.

Follow these 15 steps and never look back. Your purpose as a parent is to protect, educate, and provide for your child and that is it. Follow these guidelines and be willing to implement some of your own. Remember that rebuilding trust takes time, patience, diligence, both parties' cooperation, and consistency. You can do it.

Chapter Nine

How to Be and Stay in Control

If you believe you can handle a task, then take it on full steam, but never slack when someone is following your example.

- Cederick W. Tardy II

Control, in this chapter, has to do with control of the situations in your home, control over your son's actions, and control over your own faults to assume a true leadership role.

How much control do you want? Do you want complete and utter domination of your child? If so, this is not the book for you. Read a book on witchcraft or voodoo if your expectations are for complete control. The human will is one of the strongest forces in the universe, as strong as gravity. Total mental control is only in the movies. In real life, you will have to learn to persuade your son towards your ways of thinking.

Below are seven control points:

Number One: Be confident.

Be confident does not mean be cocky, or strut your stuff. Being confident has to do with how you think and the way you carry yourself.

Have you ever felt a little less than in the presence of your son? Have you ever felt like you act differently around your girlfriends than with your son? Does it seem like around your girlfriends or at work you are a superwoman, confident and standing tall, but when you get around your son you get confused, frustrated, and let him get the best of your patience?

It is possible and beneficial to carry that same real-world confidence that you use to relate at work or around friends, or anywhere you feel like you are on top of things, to your home. Carry yourself in a manner that exudes a self-confident vibe at home. Poke your chest out, keep your head up, speak firmly and clearly, give the impression you know what you are doing. *People respect confident people. Respected people have control.* These things have nothing to do with being mean and cocky.

Staying in Control

When you talk to your son, look him in the eyes, stand square with him, stand tall, and speak clearly. Assert yourself and exude an attitude of authority. You are just letting him know through body language that you are in charge.

Have you ever wondered why a puny football coach or boxing trainer can get a big football player or boxer to listen to his every command? It is the way that the coach or trainer carries himself. The coach may be 65 years old, but he walks, talks, and carries himself as if he will put a foot in the star player's behind without thinking twice about it. The players respect him, not because of his size, but because his self-confidence through body language says that he knows what he is doing. Your body language speaks loudly. Pick your head up, put your shoulders back, and speak clearly to your son from now on, but do not yell. Keep a firm, authoritative tone, without screaming, because then you have lost control.

Number Two: Be the source for advice.

I learned over time that human beings must have a leader in everything they do that involves more than one person. In a team sport, in a jury, in a gang, in any social situation, human beings yearn for a leader. The simple idea that someone knows a topic better then we do makes us want that person to take command.

Your son is eager for you to lead him in the home. However, know that this is where your leading will stop, until he asks for it. Leaders do not force themselves onto their followers. The followers force themselves onto the leader once they trust them. Once your son leaves the house you no longer have control. Your only control from that point on will be your voice in his head. Once your son leaves your presence, the only means you have of influencing him are by the things he remembers that you have told him. The more things you tell him, like a broken record, those things will come to his memory more often than not when faced with a thorny situation.

Lead him throughout the times you have the chance and let your words lead him when he is gone. He is yearning for you to talk to him even if it appears as if he is not listening. One of my biggest complaints with my parents, both mom and dad, were that they rarely gave me solid advice when I was growing up.

Your son, just as I was, is young and naive to a lot about life and the world. School him at home. Dedicate your time, about an hour a week at least, to *Real Life 101*, where the instructor is his mom. He will appreciate it more then he could ever believe when he moves out of the house. Your words will have to lead him. You know more about life than he does, so he will look to you for direction.

Number Three: Never let him think he is smarter than you.

In order to keep control of your boy, you should never let him think that he is smarter than you are. Granted, the things they are teaching kids in school are getting more advanced daily, but do not get disturbed by this.

If you cannot help him with his homework, remember to stay confident. Do not say, "I do not know how to do this." The smart parent who doesn't know how to assist with a math problem, for example, should encourage better listening in class, staying after school to get help from the teacher, and inviting a classmate over to study with (preferably a classmate who gets As in the subject). It wouldn't hurt to make some cookies and sandwiches either, mom.

From this, he should not feel as though he is smarter than you are, but instead he will feel as if you have actually helped him and given him some good direction and advice. *For a parent to utter the words "I do not know," means you have lost control. Avoid this answer.*

Another excellent way to help your child with his homework is to have him teach you what he has learned. This works when you already know the subject, and it is also helpful when you are clueless about the subject. Imagine this. If your son can learn the material efficiently enough to teach you how to do it correctly, he will surely be able to pass his test. Now you have bonded, learned, spent time together, and built confidence in your son.

It is my belief that you should never let a child think they are smarter than you are. Children do not understand that they will most likely never be smarter than their parents. They may know more textbook stuff, but I assure you textbooks do not help with real life. Do not tell them that though. They might disregard school as something unimportant. School is definitely important. The point is, if your kids stump you with a question, give them some kind of good advice, but never cop out with the "I don't know" answer. Once they feel they are smarter then you, it is all downhill from there. Do not let this attitude take hold, because it is hard to reverse, and devastating if left unattended. They will never want to listen again. They will think you are an idiot, and the names only get worse from there.

Number Four: Telling with force is captivating.

As a military police officer, I came to realize that when you tell someone to do something with a proper amount of force and confidence in your voice, they usually do it. This works with all age groups. The key is eye contact, body language, and the tone of voice. When all of these factors line up, the reaction from the person spoken to is compliance. It is fascinating the way people will do what you say when you tell them to instead of ask them. A leader sometimes has to voice commands instead of asking questions. For example, instead of asking, "Can you do the dishes?" Say, "Do the dishes, and have them done in 20 minutes." Remember you are not yelling, but using an authoritative tone of voice that asserts dominance.

Now this is where it gets good. I know what your question is. "What do you do if he still does not listen? Do I beat him or yell at him or what?" You do not hit him or argue with him if he does not listen.

Appeal to the emotions. Get your point across without arguing or causing more tension. You may even have to change the subject, but who cares? If you have to change the subject then do so. You control the talks, not your son. Change the subject to how you feel, and make sure he feels your pain. When it calms down, go back to the topic at hand and watch the difference in the conversation from then on. Remember to always look him in the eyes, and portray proper body language. People often forget these things during emotional and stressful situations, but no longer will you.

Stroking a man's emotions, no matter what his age, is always more effective at persuading his thoughts than messing with his ego. That is just asking for a fight. If your son does still go and do whatever it was you told him not to, if he is that bad, he was going to do it anyway whether you fought with him or not. Try this and see if it makes a difference. If you have been yelling and fighting with him until whatever age he is now, then you need to remember to give adequate amounts of time for this new attempt to work. It will not (it might), but most likely will not work the first time. I am not a magician, and this is not a rabbit-out-of-the-hat trick.

When he comes home from doing whatever foolishness he did even though you told him not to, do not jump in his face yelling and arguing about it. Just keep attacking those emotions of his until his Wall of Jericho crumbles from the power of your voice. Remember body language and tone of voice are very important, and you must keep your temper.

Number Five: Make him feel important.

No one appreciates anything more than feeling important. When you feel important you feel like you generally want to do whatever you are asked, and you will do it superbly. Make your son feel important by giving him important things to do. My mother used to let me take the Durango to the grocery store. It may seem petty, but at 15 or 16, I felt like The Man! I had the grocery list and the money too. I felt like a grown up, or like the family was depending on me to fulfill this duty. I would not smoke any weed either, because I did not want to wreck the car!

No matter what it is, let your son get a piece of the action. Let him help you tabulate the bills or something. Whatever you let him do, give him praise for it, and appreciation. Make him feel as though he has made a difference. This is when you want to positively stroke his ego. When a man feels important, he will do what he is asked.

Number Six: Do not threaten.

I am sure you know not to threaten and not follow up, but how many times do you make this mistake a month? Every time that you do, you are really just breaking your trust with your son. A threat is just a promise with a negative connotation. When you threaten him, you are promising him something, and when you do not come through it is just as if you broke a positive promise. Your son begins to feel negative self-worth.

He is thinking, "My mom doesn't even love me enough or want to spend enough time with me to follow through with her threats. She doesn't even care or worry about me enough to fulfill a threat." He is thinking something similar to this every time, whether it is consciously or subconsciously. Also, as a military police officer I learned that threats only antagonize people. Instead of making a point, you are just messing with the male ego again and asking for a fight.

Number Seven: He needs positive attention.

Positive attention will really help you stay in control of his actions in the home or in your presence. Many kids act up just to get attention. I do not know why, but they do. They do not even care if the attention is a belt as long as they are acknowledged. Next time your kid does something stupid, don't beat him. Give him something positive to walk away with from the situation. Always encourage him to do and strive for better than the average. Appeal to his emotions. Explain that if he continues to act this way, he will get lost among all of the other average people and never make it in society. Always add some sort of advice instead of inflicting verbal, physical, or mental abuse.

This type of attention is basic *positive reinforcement*. Use stories and talks like a broken record to make sure the message sticks. Many kids complain that their parents do not talk to them enough. Make him complain you talk too much! Speak positive, life-filled, knowledge-filled words to your kids daily.

I recommend rereading this chapter a few times to make sure these points stick. If you can really implement them, they will have positive affects on your family's development–without a doubt.

Chapter Ten

Once You Have Him

Getting through to a teenager is about as hard as catching a greased pig, but neither is impossible if you use the right techniques.
- Cederick W. Tardy II

  All of these tips I am giving you moms, if applied, will produce positive results. But after reaching this point comes a new battle. I stress the following point: *Once you have a hold on your son, never let it go. Once you have backed him up and gained ground, do not ever give it back.* This chapter was written to remind you of why we have all had failures in our lifetime, and to open eyes and hearts to the fact that positive changes in your son's behavior *now* do not mean he will remain that way.
  A mistake many people make in life is, they get inspired, gain a lot of ground, get comfortable, lose focus, and then lose ground. That is the tale of nearly everybody's life. They start something, do a good job, get happy, and then a few months later they have lost focus, given up and become discouraged. A majority of the population has never accomplished their dreams. Your son's life, however, is not a dream. His future is not something that you want to lose focus on.
  The majority of us work hard at something for a while, and by the next year we have forgotten about what it is we were so excited about doing. Examine your own life for traces of this behavior pattern. Have you ever gotten inspired, gained ground, grown comfortable, lost focus, and then lost all that you had gained?
  My biggest fear is that some mother will read this book, get inspired to make changes in her family, make some excellent adjustments, but then get comfortable with the way things are going and lose focus. This is my biggest fear because this will lead to her losing everything that she worked so hard for with her son's future. If you do not keep fighting you will lose the ground you once gained on the battlefield. Do you remember the saying, "You may have won the battle, but you have not won the war?" In case some of you don't know, raising teenagers is a war. I know, because I had a hell of a war with my own mother. I can't wait to see what my children will have in store for me.
  If you are not in a battle with your son right now, that is because either you

have won the battle or it has not started yet. For the latter group, your child will declare war soon, so I recommend you prepare for it now. Moreover, when you get to this war, it is not enough to win a few battles. You have to win the entire war. That could take 18 or more years. Gain ground, hold your ground, and remain victorious to win this war.

One mistake my mother made in warfare with me was she would sometimes accept my *white flags of surrender* and prematurely draw back her defenses. When I was a kid, I was good at making her believe I was sorry for what I had done when I wasn't. I would just make her feel so guilty for punishing me. This did not always work, but it worked enough times for me to feel I needed to write about it. My tactic was simply offering her a surrender plea in hopes that she would let me go. Nearly every single time I would try this, she would fall for it and let me go. As soon as she would let her guard down, I would always counterattack and take back the ground she had taken from me.

I am using this warlike imagery to enforce the fact that you are in a real fight for your son's life. These illustrations are meant to cement the idea that you are standing toe to toe with this boy. It is you versus your son in a battle for his future. If you lose that battle, it will be up to your child to determine how he should raise himself to become an adult. Think about that. A child raising himself to become an adult. Not too many kids can do that successfully. Children need guidance and instruction.

If you do not remember anything else from this book, remember that *the victory is not yours until that boy is a success and there is no chance of him turning back.*

Many books encourage you to make sudden changes and many books encourage you to be tough, but in this book, I wish to encourage you to refrain from reverting to your old ways after you have gained a certain level of success. You must be rooted like a tree. Have you ever noticed that trees never grow, then stop, and then go back to being little trees again? Trees constantly grow taller and taller.

Solidify and never give up on your accomplishments. Never look back. Because the moment you look back you take your eyes off what is coming ahead of you. With a teenage boy there will always be things coming ahead of you. You will lose ground every moment that you lose sight. *Always try to remember what it was like to be a teenager.* And then multiply that 10 times to keep up with today's teens.

Your ability to implement changes and not get complacent once you see positive results will be the difference in a temporary victory versus a lasting peace agreement. Victory goes to whoever is standing at the end of the war.

Learn to recognize *white flag of surrender* from a full resignation from past behaviors. The difference is in the attitude and the words your son will speak. You will notice a true sign of lasting change when you notice changes in the attitude of your son and changes in the words he speaks. This ties into judging his actions. If he says he is never going to do whatever he did wrong again, but is still asking to go to the same places and hang out with the same people, he has not changed. That would be merely a *white flag* to get you to lower your guard so he can escape the bondage of parental constraint.

I used to always tell my mother that my friends and I were going to go to a certain someone's house. Every time I came back from that certain someone's house, I would be high as a kite! Times changed–I got busted. I swore up and down that I was done with drugs after that. A few months later, after she relaxed her restraints, I said, "Mom, the guys and I are going to go to a certain someone's house." What do you think she should have done?

Whenever you get control, you must constrict. Like a snake grabs a rodent, you must grab, hold, and not let go until there is full compliance with no chance of regression. When you gain ground, do not give it back just because your son has been fine for a few weeks. Lasting change takes longer than a few weeks. *Change can occur in a short period, but lasting change cannot be considered "lasting change" until after it has lasted; stood the test of time.*

My mother and even my father tried everything they knew to overcome my substance addiction. Remember, I was out drinking, smoking, and popping pills for a while. They tried everything they knew, but they did not know that the one thing they needed to do was keep doing what they were doing. They gave in when I put up my *white flag*. They surrendered when I surrendered. I reverted as soon as I saw my chance of escaping the constraint of parental bondage.

I can remember exactly what happened. I got kicked out of my mother's home for all of my foolishness, and went to live with my father. When I got there, I got busted again with a nice sized bag of weed and some paraphernalia. My dad made me flush it and then he destroyed my pipes. They sent me to counseling because I would not talk to them, which worked. I was able to talk to the counselor more than I could talk to them because the counselor knew how to listen.

In my head, I figured that if I was ever going to get out of my dad's house and back to Houston, I was going to need to play along with him. I had my plan down. I went to school in his small town and did exceptionally well academically. I had nearly straight As, and I was not drinking, smoking, partying, or even going out at all. I just sat around and moped to make him feel sorry for me. This was my *white flag*. In his eyes and my mother's, I had finally surrendered, but in my head, I was working a plan. I learned a lot about life, which helped me later down the line from this experience, but at the time, I was complying as a ploy to get back to Houston.

If they would have stayed consistent with their punishment, and if they had not accepted my *white flag,* they would have corrected my problem. Instead, they gave up their ground when I looked as though I had given up mine. *They should have implemented more steps into their plan, since it was working, which would have guided me along the way.* Since I was getting good grades, they could have put me into a better school, for example. They could have applied any number of tactics to constrict even further and gain even more ground. (If they only knew back then what I am telling you now.) They did not take the opportunity to do that. They accepted my decree of surrender after only six months of good behavior.

If my parents would have stuck with their punishment and outlasted my act, they could have turned me around. Had they realized they were gaining ground, they could have kept marching forward. Since I was acting, sooner or later my acting days would have had to come to an end. From there, they could have engineered additional plans to ensure I never turned back again.

Instead, they gave me my ground back prematurely, thinking I was "all better." My plan had worked. I was free! That same night I was back at the drug house getting high. That very night I got extremely intoxicated, beaten up at a party, left stranded in an SUV in a train yard, and almost got hit by a train. I was with my old best friend, of course, and we got arrested by the police. This was one of the worst nights of my entire life. The war had started back up!

I am not blaming my parents for my stupid actions. I know every mistake that I made was due to my own ignorance. But the fact is, as a child, I did not and could not think as clearly as I do now. I needed my parent's direction. My continuous problems were to an extent my parent's fault.

Had they only known that when you make changes for the better, you are supposed to keep making changes for the better! Whenever you make progress in your child's life, you need to keep implementing better changes. Do not keep punishing him! This will not work at all! Keep him focused on new and better things constantly. Keep changing his environments. It may sound harsh, but studies on the world's greatest geniuses have shown that they all experienced multiple dramatic changes of environment as youths.

Soon your constricting will not even seem like punishment to him anymore. He will see the benefit and improvement in the quality of his life, and it will become his way of life. Too much restraint will cause him to resent you and blow up even more. But, if you let him get off the hook because he has shown a brief moment of sanity you will surely lose your ground and have to start over again. You have to find what your own middle ground will have to be. Just don't give in because he has complied for a little while. Keep him focused on the future and keep educating him on the future.

Your child is not in prison, but consider this. In prison, they do not let criminals go because they had good behavior for a moment. Criminals must have a proven record of accomplishment before they are even considered for release. And they must be interrogated over and over again by a board over an extended period of time to determine if they are fit to return to society. In your own little way, you might have to do the same thing prisons do with criminals. You might need to cross-examine your child repetitiously for an extended period to ensure his changes are not just a *white flag*.

Everything in this book may sound like overkill, but had my mother done even half of these things I would not have had to go the route I did. Thank God I went this route because I was able to come back around and use the experience to make a difference, but what if your child cannot do the same? Do you want to risk it?

Remember how I said that I simply played the role when punished, and how my parents should have waited out my good behavior to see if it was genuine? Consider this: Whatever your son's "it" is, you will have to wait "it" out. He will either show you that he truly has given "it" up, or he will show you that he was just throwing up a *white flag* to fool you. You will know true change because you will see it in his attitude, see it is his eyes, hear it in his voice, and feel it in your heart. You only have 18 or so years to turn that boy into a man who is ready to function in society.

Some of you mothers may have to play dirty to keep your children clean. You may have to use any means available and necessary. War is not pretty. The harder your opponent, the harder your defense and attack must be. You need to do what you have to do to keep your child free. Once you have him you must never let him go prematurely. Believe me, I am speaking from my own life experience.

Just think about how this sounds. Let us say that you ground your son for two weeks, and then once it is over you let him *go back* to his normal routine. *Go back?* I wish to make this point: Letting him *go back* is the same as letting him go backwards! Many wonder why their kids keep doing what they tell them not to do or regress back to old habits. It is because punishment alone does not correct faulty behavior. Punishment merely adjusts behavior for a moment. *Time and a good reason are the only two things that change behavior, and, for that fact, nearly everything.*

Things only change after time and for a reason. You have from this day until the day your son leaves your house as your time, and your reason is because you said so! I am just joking. Your reason is for his future, his benefit. Your reason is whatever it has to be, but there must be a good reason for him to change or else he will not change.

Most parents hate causing friction between them and their child, but consider this statement: The end of most types of friction is two smooth surfaces… No matter how long it takes to smooth him out, just take the time.

The hardest part is going to be finding what your child is interested in and then getting him to stay focused on it for success. The easy part is going to be changing the relationship between you and him. The relationship will change immediately the moment he understands that you love him, listen to him, and are willing to understand him. You will need to build an excellent bridge of communication. Learn from the psychologist I had to visit. I would never speak to anyone, but I spoke to her because she listened to me, and that was the difference. She knew what was good for me, but she did not try to push it on me; instead she let me speak my heart. She gained my trust and respect, and then I was open to listen. I still did not change immediately, but there was a seed planted in my heart that sprouted my desire to change.

She figured out where my mind was. In order to maintain your ground you must find out where your child's mind is. Respect his version of reality, and work from his version to real-world reality. Once you think you have him figured out, paraphrase it back to him. If you are correct, your next step is to build him a plan to follow from that day until the day he leaves your house for good. It is up to you to plan his life, not him. He is just a kid. He cannot even think past tomorrow, nor remember yesterday. Have a plan ready for him.

Wherever your son's mind is, and whatever his positive dreams are, build him a plan to get him there. If he likes music, get him lessons and the equipment he will need to be a success at music. Do not go and buy him a $50 keyboard, if he really needs a $2,000 keyboard. Instead, add into the plan for him to get a job, save his money, and then you can add your money with his money to get him that keyboard. This is teamwork with you as the team leader. You will have to be his direction or else his travel will be off the mark. A child left up to his own judgment will choose clothes and video games over tools needed to achieve a goal.

Please do not get encouraged now, and then two years later lose hope because the results you expected did not come. Rarely does anyone get exactly what he or she expected, but those who quit never ever get what they want.

Stop being scared that your child is going to hate you. Stand up for yourself. Be a parent first, not a friend. Your child will hate you more if you fail him as a parent than he will hate you for correcting him when he is wrong.

Chapter Eleven

Clams and Clam Openers

Keep an open mind in all situations, and never forget to put yourself in the other person's shoes.

- Cederick W. Tardy II

    This chapter offers clues and details to help the mother with a son who refuses to talk to her. This is not for the mother who has a quiet son, though some tips will help break even the quiet son out of his shell. This chapter is for the boy who has the complete "I do not care attitude," and shrugs his shoulders or says "whatever" every time you ask him something or tell him something. This situation is deeper then you would think. You probably know based on your own childhood experiences how your son is feeling, but remember that you are a woman and grew up in a different era. Listen to your heart, relate this chapter's message to your own episodes, and you will find the answers you have been looking for.
    There are two types of people in the world: introverts and extroverts. Introverts tend to stay to themselves, while extroverts tend to be more comfortable in social situations. Many parents have a hard time figuring out whether their child is an introvert and just quiet, or whether their child just hates talking to them. Before you make the determination that your child hates you, has suicidal tendencies, or anything drastic, determine first if it is his personality that is making him so quiet. You could cause severe damage to your son's self-esteem by telling him he is not normal because he is quiet. Do yourself the favor and have your son take a Myers-Briggs examination to discover his personality traits. Once you have an understanding of his personality, you will be able to make wise decisions about how to manage your parenting situation.
    I continue to harp on the fact that communication is the most important part of any relationship, especially the mother and son relationship. Communication, or the lack thereof, was the principal dilemma my mother and I dealt with. Without communication in the home, you will feel like you are living with a complete stranger no matter how long you have known the person. This will cause uneasy feelings, which will drive an even bigger wedge between you and your son.
    Do you ever feel like you cannot get past "Hello" without causing tension be-

tween you and your son? Often your intentions are as harmless as wanting to know how his day was, but, somehow a simple question like this becomes an all-out fight, resulting in both of you arguing, and someone saying something in the heat of passion that they do not really mean. This argument causes scars and pain that only time can heal, but you do not have time. You have a job, or two, or three, bills, a headache, a boyfriend, and whatever else. You have to stop the problem now. Communication is your key.

Your problem is that you want to talk to your son, but he does not want to talk to you. Why does he not want to talk to you? Often it is because you do not know how to talk to him. My mother did not know what to say to me or how to talk to me. The result was that I withdrew, not to be mean, but to protect myself from getting mad at a remark that could rub me wrong. If your boy has this type of personality, you will really have to work to have a decent conversation with him. This personality does not mesh well with everyone. You have to be willing to work with your boy if he has this aloof kind of personality. It is simple to work around once you understand what the problem is, and it is worth the work, believe me.

When I was young and going through my serious *dumb days*, my mother could not get a word out of me. I would talk to her about 20 minutes a week, honestly. Imagine the huge wedge that was between us. For years we hardly spoke. Talk about a stranger in your home! We did not know anything about each other. I would talk a lot around my friends, but I was quiet at school, quiet at church, and quiet around most other people. On the other hand, I would go to parties with thousands of people, concerts, the beach, house parties, and be a wild and crazy extrovert. How do you explain this type of behavior?

Think about this: I would only talk about things I cared about, and to those who were willing to talk about what I cared about. The things I cared about were money, drugs, guns, and making money with guns and drugs. I cared about other things too, but most of the time those were the thoughts running through my head. My mother, being a Christian, was not someone who was going to sit down with me and talk about money, drugs, guns, and making money with guns and drugs. Therefore, we had nothing to talk about. She would ask me about my day, but I had nothing to tell her. I had to keep my mouth shut around her.

Your son may only want to talk about girls, sex, gangs, parties, fashion, music, sports or something you cannot relate to. Because you can't relate, he won't talk. If this is your kid's problem, your situation may need professional help. You will also need to look at talking to your kid's friends instead of trying to talk to your kid. Invite all the hoodlums over to the house. Deal with the loud talking, music, and whatever else, except guns and drugs, or total disrespect of your home. When you get the chance, pull one of them aside and talk to them about your concerns with your son. Possibly the friend will be willing to help. There still are some good kids in this world, believe me. You will be able to spot them in the crowd.

No matter what is causing your son to be so quiet around you, your number one job will need to be to understand what is going on. If your son will not talk then you need to look to other resources. This book is one resource, but you will need more case specific resources such as his favorite TV shows, his style of clothes, his styles of music, books he reads, video games he plays, friends he talks to, girls he dates, anything. Let his actions speak for him.

I call the boys who refuse to talk clams since it is so hard to open them up. The second reason I call them clams is that many clams have pearls inside of them. Being a case of a clam with a pearl inside of him myself, I am telling you there are more of us out there who are just waiting for that one person to take the time and use the right approach to open us up.

Clams, or boys who refuse to open up and talk, usually have a common trait– they are frightened and confused about the future. Teenagers are the worst when it comes to these traits, because they innately know their youthful time is running out. They realize the day is fast approaching when they will have to move out of the home and be on their own. This scares them, no matter how much BIG talk they spout off. Consider it something similar to a grown man reaching midlife crisis in terms of the sheer magnitude. It is a teenage life crisis. Your son is facing the biggest thing he has ever had to face–becoming an adult!

Scared and perplexed, your son will try his best to assume an air of confidence and independence, but inside of his teenage brain, the reality that he still needs you is screaming. He wants to be independent and prove that he is a grown up, but he knows that without you right now he would be lost, homeless, hungry, and in a heap of trouble. He wants to show an air of masculinity, but at the same time, (in a whimpering voice) he needs his "mommy." This is one reason why a teenage boy will suddenly become a clam around his mother. His quietness is his attempt to show you that he does not need you anymore, because he no longer has to talk to you or ask you for advice. He wants to disconnect his need for you so he reverts to not talking to you. Consider it the worst defense mechanism ever, but that is all he knows right now. Never forget that he is just a boy, nothing more and nothing less than a boy.

Let me add this, and please make sure you are taking this down in your notes. The boys who express and really stress the craving for independence from their mothers the strongest are most often the worst off. These boys are the dumb ones, sorry to say. I was one of these dumb ones. Dumb is a harsh word, so let me say extremely naïve instead. The boys who are always pulling away are the ones who will wind up in a jail cell or at rock bottom soon because they never took the time to learn from their mothers. They are the most confused, selfish, lost, ungrateful, naïve, unaware of the future, and bewildered boys of them all. Don't be fooled by their air of confidence!

These boys will need the most hand-holding, no matter how hard they pull away. There is a big difference between an intelligent walk away, and an arrogant, prideful, naïve rip away from the mother. I strongly recommend you do not let your son pull away before he is ready. Despite his macho, brutish attitude, he will need a great deal of supervision, guidance, and assistance. The logical boys will succeed with little or no supervision, but not the irrational brutes. The boys who are willing to listen to you or someone with some sense, willing to learn, willing to ask for help, and do not mind asking how something works will graduate from youth to be wonderful prodigies.

Plant these character traits in your son: willingness to listen to you or someone with some sense, willingness to learn without embarrassment, and willingness to ask for help. The boys with these characteristics at an early age will have the tools needed to become a success. The brutish, macho boys who never change will either land their butts in jail or hit rock bottom. Hopefully they have a life-changing experience; certainly let's hope for more than rock bottom for these children.

Let me be honest with you, mothers. Having the clam-like personality that I had as a teenager hurt me so much as a young adult. I overcame some major, astronomical, exorbitant issues of depression, loneliness, feelings of rejection, and everything in between to be where I am now. It was no easy task. It took lots of soul searching, trusting in God, being honest with myself, and begging others to be honest with me to dig myself out of the hole I was in.

As I explained in the introduction, I went an entire semester at school without talking. If I talked, it was extremely rare. This quickly became easy for me to do, so I carried this wall around with me, everywhere. Going through my no-talking stage was damaging to me as a person. While other teenagers were dating and making lasting friendships, I was sitting in a corner with a pencil, a note pad, a CD player, a drug addiction, and a brain that was full of anger. I slowly began to relate only to myself. The worst thing I ever did was convince myself that I was intelligent, when I wasn't. I began holding everyone to unobtainable standards, driving everyone from me. I was alone.

If your son is doing these things, correct the problem as soon as possible. Your son has to get out into the world for his own good. A phase of quietness is normal, but when it becomes who he is, you need to seek professional help. I was literally wallowing in myself. I became all I knew.

The effect became noticeable when I joined the Navy. I didn't know how to talk to people or how to relate with various types of people. If I were to judge my people skills from one to 10, with 10 being the best, a three would have been an overstatement in my case. I do not want to sound as though I was a complete hermit for my whole life. I want to express the fact that the one semester I spent in silence was long enough to make the silent behavior a habit. A terrible habit.

I've said this to amplify the fact that your son going for a long period without talking is more detrimental to his future than he could have a clue about. The reason that he may choose to revert to silence may or may not be for the same reasons I did, *but the harm will be the same.* It is your job to not let him fall into that trap, and be sure that he understands this. His refusal to have a discussion is a rejection of life and all that it can provide through conversation.

Never forget that he is a boy, nothing more and nothing less. Also, never forget how confused he is dealing with masculinity and childhood. Compare it to the magnitude of a midlife crisis. Remember that by temperament, his actions are possibly natural if he is an introvert, but if the scenario is severe and plays out for a long period, you may need to consider seeking professional assistance. I strongly recommend that before you go to sleep tonight or before you put this book down for the day that you read the chapter on listening barriers and tips.

You have to be willing to understand that your son is not the sole problem. There are two of you in this duet, which means that the two of you are the problem. Since both of you are the problem, both of you will have to work it out cooperatively. This goes for every circumstance and especially for communication. Communication is a two-way street, not an invasive grilling. I recommend that you quickly learn to familiarize yourself with your son's culture, whatever that may be. Figure out who he is. *Once you know who he is, you will know how to talk to him, and once you know how to talk to him, he will be willing to learn how to talk to you.* With this relationship your words can have an impact on his thinking.

Rebuilding your relationship will not happen completely in one night, week, month, or even one year in some circumstances. It takes personal growth and a total attitude adjustment to make this process work. This is the only true way to make it work. Communication is the only way to rebuild what has been torn down. Communicating is the only way to learn about the boy in the other room. Whether by voice, letters, or e-mail, you need to communicate, and communicate often.

Communication is more than casual chitchat, parents. Communication is more than talking about work, school, and the day's events. Communication is building a relationship and sharing personal questions and emotions. Many of you are trying to hold watercooler-type conversations with your children, and wondering why it is not working. Your son is not an acquaintance from work. He is your son. He can tell when you are not being sincere and this will give him an uneasy feeling about you, causing him to clam up. He wants more from you than a couple of questions about his day. He wants to be able to express himself to you. He just does not know how, and he does not know if he can without you getting riled up if he says something you do not agree with. It is thoughts and feelings like these that flow through his mind, causing him to clam up.

In order to open your clam, you first need to open yourself. You need to be an open book, just as I have tried to be in this book. You need to be able to tell your son things that you have never told anyone else. One thing I criticized my mother about when I got older was how I never really felt I knew her. She rarely told me anything about who she was, or how she became who she was.

A little advice before you attempt to tell your son everything about yourself: Do not do it all at once. Space these types of conversations out, because some of the things you will tell him are going to blow his little mind away.

Use this approach when you have no idea what to say to him. If you two are driving in the car and listening to music, turn the music down and tell him about the music you used to listen to when you were his age and see if you can find a radio station that is playing something from your era. He might look at you weird, but that is okay, trust me. *It is when he does not even consider looking at you at all that you have a problem. If he continues to stare out the car window, ignoring you, then you have a problem. Get professional help!*

Music is only a small portion of what you have to talk about. You have years and years of life experiences to share with him that are packed full of wisdom. Many mothers worry about what age they should start telling their child certain things about life. My opinion is, as soon as he can understand the basic concepts of English, you should be teaching him everything about life that you know. Treat yourself like a cassette tape. Press rewind or flip the tape over and make him listen to everything all over again. Never stop talking. Do not worry about whether or not he can handle the things you will be telling him. He hears worse stuff at school, in music, and on TV than you will probably ever say to him.

Search yourself for the right things to say, and if you are a praying woman, then pray about things to say to him. Think through conversations ahead of time. Plan and know what you are going to say and how you are going to say it before you say it. *Say the things that make your stomach get the butterflies when you say them.* Tell your son about your first boyfriend or first date. Talk about fights you have won and lost, your grades and conduct in school, and parties you went to in school. Tell your son about the craziest things you have ever seen and done, your favorite cars, the good and bad times of your life, and your favorite books and movies.

There is so much to talk about. Tell him about things you have learned along the way, positive experiences, your parents, your first job, your first house, tragic events in history you were alive to witness, and everything you can. This is when you are truly being an open book. Being an open book is one approach to opening a clam. Every mother will have to develop her own approaches that coincide with her personality.

Another approach you can use is the invasive approach. Do this in a comical way only. By this I mean, walk into your son's room with a big tray of finger foods, or fruit, sit down somewhere, place the food between you two and just start talking to him. He will probably be upset the first time, but he will get over it. If it works out to be a good idea, you have created a snack meeting with your son that you could do regularly.

A different approach is adapting the appeals and approaches that you use. Every time you ask for something you are making an appeal, but the way you make the appeal is what really matters the most. There are emotional appeals, argumentative, apologetic, livid, logical, and rational appeals. The list goes on for as long as you want it to. You need to learn how to use these appeals for your benefit. Maximize your range of appeals. This will take a lot of conscious thought though, and many parents will never consider using this approach even though it is effective. When you learn how to press someone's buttons with different appeals, you can turn them off and on.

An alternative approach is openly admitting to your son that you are sorry for how you have been as a parent up until this point. Express to him that now you understand what you were doing wrong and you have vowed to make the appropriate changes to correct any deficiencies that you had in the past. Explain to him that you are really focusing on making the relationship between the two of you better, and ask for his cooperation. Ask him if he would be willing to "check you" if you start to backslide, and let him know you will be doing the same with him. It will be hard for your son to take all of this at once so let him adjust slowly. Your sole goal in life after you say something as big as this will be to never draw back on your word. He will surely hold you accountable whether he says it aloud or not. Once he knows you can be trusted, he will open up easily. Be sure that you intimately study the chapter on rebuilding trust.

There are so many ways to open a clam, and like I said, you may not be able to use any of the ideas in this book, but please use your heart and create your own ideas that work for your situation.

Another way to open a clam is to write letters. These can be e-mailed or even handwritten. I recommend handwritten. Imagine how your son would feel if he went to check the mail and found a sweet card or letter from his mother mailed to him. Drop the letter at the post office, put it in the mailbox addressed to your son or leave it where you know he will find it.

One of my personal favorite clam openers is the "third-person approach." The third-person approach is realizing that more often than not, people feel more comfortable talking to someone else about their problems than they do talking to the person with whom they have the problem. To use this approach it would be wise to use a counselor or some other professional for confidentiality or privacy reasons. Another way to use the third-person approach could be talking to your son's friends, teachers, counselors at school, football coach, and so forth. They can give you a lot of insight into his true behavior, his behavior outside of the house.

Now that you have a general idea of some ways to open a clam, let me describe things that cause him to clam up.

Whenever your son does approach you with something sensitive, please do your best to refrain from cutting him off, talking over him, asking him questions while he is talking and giving advice immediately. All of these things separately will cause him to clam up, and if you find yourself doing all of these things already, then you see why you have a clam on your hands!

You should always teach your son and give him advice, but sometimes you need to take an indirect approach to keep from hurting his pride, which will cause him to clam up. I know it is hard as a mother to watch your son struggle through simple problems that you have the answer to, but sometimes you have to stand back and let him figure them out on his own, if they aren't life threatening. He needs to figure out how to either work through the problem himself, or ask for help, but do not consistently provide him the answers. He will become accustomed to your help and grow lazy and dependent on you forever. Instead of giving advice right away, ask him questions like, "What are you going to do about that?" or "What is your point of view?" Lead him into the answer. Let him think on his own. Once he figures out that he needs your help he will ask for it, but until then, just try your best to direct him to the right answer.

Boys tend to clam up whenever someone is very forceful with them. This brings into play a pride issue, and activates the aggressive tendency within him. Whenever a male feels threatened he gets quiet and clams up in preparation to defend himself. It is wise for you to avoid forcing him to talk.

Avoid playing the "who has it the worst game" with your child. This refers to conversations when you argue about who had a harder life, a rougher day, and all that. You have it tougher than your child does, but arguing with him is not going to solve anything. Arguing with him is only going to cause him to put another item on his list for the next "who has it worse" argument. Arguing will surely cause your boy to clam up.

Also, be consistent in your parenting. If you start something today and by the end of the day you change your mind, your son is going to be looking at you, wondering what is going on with you. Be consistent. A good rule of thumb is to try something for a month or two and then judge its effectiveness.

When my mother requested that I write a chapter specifically for "How to talk to the boy who will not talk," I do not think this is what she had in mind. I think she wanted simple step-by-step, tried and tested truths, but that is impossible to do. Everyone is different. Instead, I did my best to open your eyes to the possible mistakes you could be making, and several ways to avoid and correct them. In my own opinion, this approach is much more valuable than any 10-step program.

Remember not to rush into any hasty judgments, please, because some kids are just quiet kids. This chapter is not designed to approach the quiet kid, although some of the approaches could very well work. With that being said, I feel obliged to mention a few approaches for getting the normal quiet kid to talk as well.

Kids who are naturally quiet are usually quiet because either they lack self-confidence or they have nothing to say. This kid needs one thing in life. He needs to experience it. For the natural quiet kid with low self-esteem, I highly recommend that you get him interested in traveling, get him involved in summer camps, youth sports, or anything active and social. Get him out into the world as much as you can. This kid needs to experience life so he can have something to talk about. Sitting around at home playing video games in his room is not going to open him up and help him succeed. Do not take his video games away from him, as this would cause him to clam up due to anger. Instead, take his downtime from him. Take him out into the world whenever possible.

If video games are his fancy, you could also try getting involved in video games, but remember that your son needs more friends than just his mother to grow into a well-rounded young man. You could get involved in his video games by taking him to the best video game stores in your town, exploring the store with him, and learning the culture of video games. Talk to store clerks about the newest and hottest games out, or look on Google.com for advice on games and stores in your area. I even suggest that you buy a game for yourself as well as your son, and do your best to invest 45 minutes a couple of times a week to playing video games with your son. Do whatever you can to show him that you are making an effort to truly be there for him. If he does not respect it now, he will in the future.

Video games are not the only things that you can get involved in. Parents need to be involved in whatever their kid is involved in. Video games are just an example, but you may have to get involved in car shows, Future Farmers of America meetings, dance classes, the gym, or even firearm-related activities as my parents did with me.

When your son has something to do, something to talk about, and you get involved in it with him, even the quiet kid will suddenly find his words per day rising well above his norm. In time, he will break free from his shell, and he will respect you and love you for helping him through those rough times. Just force this kind of kid to get out in the world. Compel him to volunteer, read books, go to the mall, and things of this nature.

To conclude this chapter, I wish to leave you with four last tidbits and pointers.
- Talk to other parents about their silent teenagers to see if they were able to succeed in opening them up. Collect knowledge from them about how to deal with your boy.
- Do not get frustrated thinking you are the only one trying to make things work.
- Do not ever settle for shoulder shrugs and "I do not know" for answers, but also do not try to force an answer. Use a tactful and tactical approach this time around. You will be amazed at the results.
- Comedy is one of the best ways to open a clam.

Chapter Twelve

Just Give Him a Toy and He Will Be Fine

You can give a child a toy, but do not toy with them.

- Cederick W. Tardy II

In this chapter, the real "winners" of the parenting world are brought into the spotlight. Notice the sarcasm. Have you ever heard someone tell you that in order to get their kids to shut up they give them a toy? Have you ever been this parent? This chapter is meant to do one thing and one thing only, arouse a feeling of guilt in the hopes of committing an attitude for change.

You only have to change something if it doesn't work. Giving your kids a toy to get them out of your hair does not work. One day, I happened to be caught in a conversation about parenting. Being the person I am, I decided I would take notes because I knew I might run across something valuable for use in my book. What I heard that day were disgusting attempts of parents sharing their parenting tactics.

One parent told another parent that the best way to keep their kids occupied is to buy them a trampoline! What? Buy your kid a trampoline to keep them occupied? Whatever happened to spending time with your kids? Since when did TV and toys become more important then your child's development? I was astonished when I heard this. The parent's logic was that by the time night falls, the kids are so tired that they just eat dinner, shower, and go to sleep. Sound familiar?

Have you ever *made* your kids play with toys so you can concentrate on something else? Have you ever bought your boy a video game system with the *intent* of it keeping his attention?

I have no problem with the parent going off to do something else, but while you are doing something else, give your kids something a little more mentally stimulating than a trampoline! Did you know the environment a child's brain develops in determines the brain's ability to function in the future? A brain that is put through more mental exercise in its early developmental stage will be better equipped for learning and thinking. An exercised brain has the ability to think quicker and will not tire so fast. A brain that is active will build more synapses and form a more advanced cerebral cortex, which is where the memory is stored.

How mentally stimulating is a trampoline, a box of Hot Wheels, a room full of action figures, a trunk full of Legos, a box full of logs, or a closet full of water guns?

Some parents sit their kids in front of a TV from afternoon until it is time to go to sleep. The same parent does not entertain his or her own children more than seven hours a week. Some parents treat their kids like a cactus. They only remember to take care of them when they get around to it, because after all, a cactus does not need too much attention–it can take care of itself. The average parent thinks that TV is educational. The average parent sees nothing wrong with a mentally dull home. The average parent has no idea how much the environment affects the development of the brain.

These "just give them a toy" parents have no idea how much their children suffer. Their idea of parenting is putting on *Scooby Doo* and letting Scooby occupy their child's time until the babysitter gets to the house. Parents with this attitude either do not know or do not care that *Scooby Doo* is not going to get their children a scholarship into a good college. *Scooby Doo* is not going to make your son successful in life. *Scooby Doo* is only going to mentally stunt his mind from growing at a time when his brain is the ripest. The younger the brain, the better suited it is for growth and development.

Instead of giving your kid a trampoline, try taking him to an art festival. Did your eyebrows rise? Yes, take him to an art festival. Give him a chance to see colors, ask questions, and explore different cultures. Take your child to do all sorts of activities that you think might be mentally expanding. The more stimulating the environment and the more diverse the experiences the brain undergoes while developing, the stronger, healthier, and smarter the brain will become.

My mother forced me to try different venues and volunteer events. I hated every second of every one, but I know why she did it now. She knew that she had to get me away from the TV. She knew she had to get me away from the monotonous dull drag of normalcy. She knew she had to take my hands from the controllers of the *Play Station*. Now I can look back and see how much it forced me to grow. If we had only kept at it, how far ahead would I be?

Mothers, you have the responsibility to keep your kid occupied in something, and that something might as well be educational. I do not believe that you have to make your child read the dictionary or volumes from the encyclopedia, but you can try various other things to educate him. Remember that unless your child has been raised living a life of education, this mentally stimulating approach will seem foreign to him. If you wish to make this change permanent, you will have to make each step a gradual one. Trying to push a book at a kid who is only used to watching TV is not the easiest thing to do. He will only push it right back at you, or better yet, leave it sitting right where you left it.

THE BIG PAYBACK

I suggest doing your best to get your son out in the world for the purpose of exploring, even if all you can do is take him to the park to play with other kids. You do not have to be rich to explore. Exploration is doing what you do not normally do. If normally you watch TV all day on the weekends and your kid sits in his room watching TV, then break that cycle. Plan a mini vacation.

If you do not have money for a mini vacation, then take him to the museum. In areas like Houston, places like the NASA Space Museum are excellent. Go to a library with him and spend a good amount of time finding a book that the two of you can agree on. Check out the book and read it together. Another idea of interest might be any type of festival, as I have mentioned. Festivals are great places to learn new and exciting things and they are not very expensive.

These are ideas that are not expensive. If you have money then of course you are afforded bigger and better things, but money does not always produce a good time. Many things that are fun are also free. Many things are educational that cost nothing more than time. The best things, of course, are things that neither you nor your child has ever done before. Try going hiking, horseback riding, shooting, fishing, bike riding, tree climbing or golfing. Of course, these are all things I would want to do. Whatever you think that both of you could do that is new to you, do it. Newness and creativity always lead to mental expansion.

I recommend that you frequently do something that your son wants to do. Let him plan a weekend. His weekend may be exaggerated, but as long as it is all in good taste and worthwhile, roll with it. At least you are doing something worthwhile with your son, that is fun for him, mentally expanding, and it gets both of you out of the house. This is better than a trampoline anytime.

A toy is not sufficient, moms. I sincerely believe *GI Joe* will not teach your son how to become a man. Parents need stop looking at their kids as a nuisance. Become proactive in expanding your son's mind while he is young. You have the chance to show him what the world has to offer. *If you forfeit the chance to help him expand now, then you forfeit the chance to demand expansion later.*

Exposure to exciting and mentally stimulating ideas will broaden your son's capability to grasp new tasks when he is older in life. *His environment now is, in all actuality, determining the environment he will stick close to when he is older.* He will only stick close to what he finds comfortable when he grows up and moves away from you. If he is comfortable with the new and exciting then he will always be well outfitted in life.

Chapter Thirteen

Overcoming a Single Mother's Financial Struggles

Handling your money is not hard to do once you realize how important it is. Cut back and save where you can, and do the best to make more money with what you have.

- Cederick W. Tardy II

I spent some time pondering my life, thinking about what else I needed to add to this book. What else could I have and would I have changed in my life had I known better? I thought about tears shed in a dark house trying to do my homework by candlelight. I thought about the many nights I went to bed hungry because we ate the last of the oatmeal the day before. I thought about pushing our car down the street because it ran out of gas. I thought for a while and realized what I was missing.

Statistics state that the majority of single African-American mothers are raising their children in conditions considered below the poverty line. After thinking about my own life, and reminiscing about my friends who lived with their moms, I began to see a pattern. I do not want to paint a picture that I was malnourished, dead poor, or even that I was lacking anything. The incidents I named above happened, but they did not happen every single day.

This is by no means a finance book, but someone reading this has no idea what she can do for her kids besides get on welfare or work three jobs. It is not impossible to supply the needed provisions to produce a successful family.

As I stated earlier, our family experienced financial challenges. I believe many of those challenges could have been avoided by having a standard financial plan. We had money, but we spent it all, all the time, way too fast. Have you ever had this problem? You get paid, pay the bills, buy what you want, and then some unforeseen needs show up, but there is not enough money. That was our problem. When we had money, we were eating steak and lobster, shrimp and other delicacies, but once the money was gone after a week or so, we were back to hungry nights. Money was mismanaged.

What are your money issues? Are you a mother living beyond her means? Money, or the lack of it, is often a single mother's number one struggle. Whether it is making money or holding on to the money that she has made, there is difficulty. If this sounds familiar please keep reading.

Many times my mother worked more than one job to provide for us. She would work from early in the morning until way past midnight. No matter how many jobs she had though, there was never a surplus of cash. In fact, things seemed to get worse. I knew another kid whose mother resorted to becoming a stripper to provide for the family. She even got fake breasts! As boys, we didn't complain at all about his mom being a stripper or having fake breasts, but now as a young man, I see that situation completely differently.

Had either of our mothers learned how to manage their money properly, and take on a few years of purposeful discomfort and sacrifice, neither that boy I spoke of nor I would have missed many years of meaningful relationships with our mothers. There is a big difference between working hard for your family and working hard in the family. Both are important, yes, but what good is a family that has everything, except for their mother?

Had our mothers only learned the importance of budgeting strictly, saving as much money as possible, living below what a salary can provide, investing, owning a home, maintaining a good credit score, and so on, things would have been dramatically different. All of those things I just named, if you are not doing any of them, then you are missing out on a better quality of life that is possible for all of us. You do not have to be rich to own anything; you just have to be willing to pay the price. Everything has a price. Being poor has its price. *Being ignorant has a heavy price.*

Please do not think that I am bashing my mother. My mother did an excellent job providing for me. She did an excellent job making sure I knew what nice restaurants were like. But, after you have just spent $75 or $100 on two people for one meal, you begin to think about what else the money could have been spent on. Maybe your problem is not frivolous spending, but wasting money on things such as cigarettes and alcohol.

What if our mothers had learned the importance of financial planning? My mother had what I would consider a well-paying job. She made enough money to live in Texas, but it was what happened once the check came in that made life hard. Some mothers do not have it as well as she did though. They do not have well-paying jobs. Many mothers are trying to support more then one kid off a minimum wage salary. Where is the help for you?

Your help comes by way of some of the positive things my mother did to improve our situation. Continue your education past a high school level. A high school graduate will generally make more money than someone who never graduated from high school, and a college graduate will generally make a great deal more money than a high school graduate.

My mother did not have her bachelor's degree at that time, but she did attend college consistently. Between working and raising a son, she was at school late at night doing her best to get an education to get that promotion she needed to put more food on the table. Additionally, she did not settle for just any job. She got a good job.

On top of that, she made sure she was always reading books, staying educated, and up-to-date with the current knowledge level. She gradually learned how to manage money once she got a part-time job with a major financial institution. She taught me the importance of investing and saving money from that point on. Finally, she did her best to own a house despite what the credit ratings may have shown. If you are living in an apartment, check the local mortgage rates in your area, and determine whether a house note would be significantly more expensive than your rent. Chances are that the house may even cost you the same or less than your apartment. Just remember, your first house, like your first car, does not have to be breathtaking. It is the first not the last. So do not break your back for that brand new two- or three-story home.

As I said before, the problem with our finances was that our priorities were all out of order. Be on familiar terms with the difference between a want and a need. A want is something that can wait forever and not really matter either way. Things like high-end basketball shoes or jewelry are wants. Whether you have them or not is not a real issue.

A need is something that cannot wait. Your hair, no matter how important it is to you, is not a need. You do not need to get your hair done every week. Needs are house payments, groceries, and utilities. The cable bill is a want, and, as a matter of fact, a television is a want. I would go so far as saying that if you are having problems keeping the lights on in your house, you do not need a TV. Instead of watching TV, read and work on finding a new source of income to keep the lights on.

For years we were living on that fine line called paycheck-to-paycheck. Whenever one little mix up was thrown into the otherwise crazy mess, things went kaput. *Put priorities first.* A good way to handle your money is to learn to live off about 60 percent of the actual money you earn. My personal budget looks something like this: Off the top, I give 10 percent to my church. Second, I put at least 10 percent into my first savings account, which I consider my in-case-something-pops-up savings account. Then I place another 10 percent into my actual savings account. The last 10 percent goes into my investment account. That is money that I am saving and investing in the stock market. Automatically I end up with only 60 percent of my paycheck to spend after the first day. It was excruciating and almost ascetic at

first, but it got easier and more enjoyable with every paycheck.
This structure offers me more good opportunities than you would realize. Giving away 10 percent to church used to be a struggle for me, but I learned how awesome it could actually be for me financially. Besides the spiritual aspects of the giving, the money I give, and any money you give to any charity, can be considered as a tax write off. Technically you end up getting the money back. The money you are saving has not gone anywhere. It is still right there for you to use if need be, but you usually do not ever need it. The money in the retirement account never gets touched. It just keeps growing and growing in the stock market. Once I learned to live off 60 percent of my income, I did not have to worry about unexpected bills. I had built a nice buffer zone between paychecks that really worked.

My recommendation for mothers is to first learn to put away "some money" into a savings account. Even if only $20 a month, just put it in the bank and forget about it. Soon enough it will grow and excite you. You will learn that it is just as easy to live without those $20. When you can, move your savings amount up. I started off only saving $50 every payday, $100 a month. You can do it too.

Another suggestion is that you move into an area where the cost of living is significantly lower. Picking up and leaving is not an option for everyone, but if you are living in an area that costs way too much, consider relocating. Always plan ahead, line up a job, a school for your son, and a place to live before you leave. For example, if you live in California, you can consider moving to somewhere like Texas for a few years. The cost of living difference will shock you. You can save thousands of dollars a year just by relocating. If you live in an area that is already considered to be low on the cost of living scale, consider some of the other options stated later on.

With relocating, consider moving near a large metropolitan city. Live near the city, but live in the outskirts where it is usually less expensive. You can easily get a good paying job in a growing metropolitan city. This allows you to make the big-city dollars, while paying small-town prices.

Whatever your final decision, you must understand the importance of a strong financial plan. You can read books or even consult a financial planner to guide your monetary decisions. I recommend books and doing it yourself, personally, because financial planners are usually not free. You can learn the same things from a book for a fraction of the cost of a planner. But, if you are not disciplined enough to budget your own funds, get a financial planner. Just make sure your planner has something to show for themselves. Your financial planner and their office should look like their finances have been well planned.

As a single mother, you must understand how important it is to manage your money properly. There are more books for handling money than there are ways to get into debt. I recommend grabbing a few of them and getting hot on fixing your credit score, debt level, and financial intelligence.

In less then 30 minutes roaming around the Internet I learn more about anything than I ever learned in high school. Maybe because I rarely paid attention in high school? Nevertheless, the point is that the information is right there for us all. You can learn almost anything on the Internet. And everything is right there for you, most of the time for free. Search Google to find out about nearly everything that has ever been found out about. All you have to do is search. This will be the most beneficial scavenger hunt of your life.

What if you do not have Internet access? Easy. Not having the Internet at home is no excuse. There are public libraries, Internet cafes, friends with computers, computers at work, and so on that you can easily use to do your research. You have to be willing to pay the price.

Whatever you find, whether it be welfare or grants, take advantage of it for your son's benefit. Put your pride down for the short-term, and take what is freely given to you. I am by no means an advocate of people riding welfare until they die. I see welfare as a crutch, not a life-support system. Limp along on welfare until your financial situation has healed and then get back out on the playing field. Do it for your son. Let him see a real-life story of the underdog making it.

There are many ways to get support and just as many ways to save money. I mentioned earlier that tax write-offs pay off big. Research different tax write-offs and utilize them to the max. Look into something as simple as a ROTH IRA, individual retirement account, and use that as a tax shelter for your money. You can research a 529 or educational savings account for your son to put him through college, which is an excellent investment. Anything that is tax deductible, maximize it, and remember not to blow your refund check. Instead, invest it.

Start saving money. Save even if you can only save $20 or $30 a week. Even these small amounts add up to hefty sums when you do not subtract from them. Learn how to invest in the stock market. It is not just for rich Caucasians anymore. The stock market has opened up to everyone, and become increasingly easier to get involved in. The profit potential is uncapped, but so is the risk. You can start investing with as little as $100, but more is better. Learn to invest in any investment vehicle that you wish, and then stick with it until it produces profit. Once you have investing down, teach your son how to invest. In so doing, you not only have educated him, but you have groomed an investment partner you can trust. Call it a mother and son hobby if you like, but call it a "need."

Look into buying a home instead of renting or leasing. After all, you have to pay to live somewhere. You might as well be paying to own. Despite your current credit score, continue looking for a home. Homes offer tax benefits, and homes almost always increase in value. A home is a sound investment. Think about this as an option. You can move into a less expensive neighborhood, purchase a house, gain equity, sell and cash out, roll the money into another property, and then do it again in another neighborhood. Do that for seven years, correcting your credit glitches as you go, and by the end of those seven years, you will have done wonders for your financial status. After you cash out of your home you can invest the money, save it or buy a new house, but don't blow it. Meanwhile you could be going to college, investing, educating your son on investing, collecting government support where you can, taking advantage of all your resources, and completely turning your life around in a matter of years.

It will not be easy, but neither is being broke and unhappy. In no time, a dedicated person could easily turn their poverty-stricken family into a middle or even upper class, Suburban-driving family, and all it takes is planning and dedication. I learned a while back that it is wiser to be uncomfortable for a short while and execute plans to reach a level of comfort, than to sit around complaining and hoping. Do you want to do better? Do you want your son to see you make something out of yourself? Do you want to provide the best for him without struggling forever? Did you know it is possible? What is stopping you? You can do it if you want to.

Once you do get a home, or if you have a home, look into renting out a room. I do not recommend renting to family or friends. Always use contracts and keep the law in your favor. There are risks of course, but the benefits are astronomical for a single mother.

Look for a roommate on the Internet from a site like: www.coabode.com. In addition, check your local newspaper, church, YMCA, at work, community center, or daycare for a prospective roommate. You may find another single mother looking for a financial break who would make the perfect roommate. Look for quality single mothers as roommates. Adding a roommate can cut your living costs in half, and you have a part-time babysitter right in the house, which cuts your bills down dramatically. Along with cutting these expenses you can continue budgeting, saving, investing, writing things off on taxes, and cutting back on other expenses. You can literally end up saving thousands!

The question now is: What do you do with all the money that you save? Well, you do not drink it away, smoke it away, sex it away, party it away, club it away, or spend it on frivolous trinkets. You save it. Build a buffer. A buffer is three to six months of income, at least. Just think about how implementing the previous paragraph in your life could make a big difference…

If you cannot find a single mother to share expenses with, you can always check local college listings for students who would be willing to rent a room at a reduced price for providing babysitting care and/or tutoring. All you have to do is contact your local college office and start from there. Now you are a homeowner, gaining property value, saving money on childcare, saving money all around the board, going to college, investing, and turning rags to riches. You can do it. You could easily be saving thousands and making thousands by the end of the year. The hardest part of any of these suggestions will be convincing yourself that they are possible.

I have another pointer for saving money. Avoid getting a pet! Pets are as expensive as kids are sometimes, and if you are strapped for cash, the last thing you need is a 70-pound dog eating you out of house and home. I can remember many days when my dog had food in the pantry and I didn't. I was envious. I always told him, "If you were not around we could have used that money to buy us some food." He never replied, but I am sure he was thankful. Save your money for now, and when things are settled, get a dog. Get two or three if you want to, but a dog is definitely a want, not a need.

As I said earlier, anything you want to learn is on the Internet right now, waiting for you to read it. One day I pulled up a website with hundreds of different money-saving tips that I implemented into my life immediately. Simple things. Saving three or four dollars here and there really adds up if you do not spend it on something else. On a military salary, I had to learn how to properly manage my money if I was ever going to be able to separate successfully. I implemented a financial plan and was able to save well into the five figures, while going to college full time, driving a brand new car, and traveling to all the spots I always wanted to on a junior military salary. I found out that everything has a price, and ignorance has a heavy price.

Chapter Fourteen

Parental Teamwork

When you begin to feel it in your heart and know it in your mind, whatever it is, go for it, and you will achieve it.

- Cederick W. Tardy II

Parental teamwork. Parents working together and combining their efforts for the benefit of all involved. How easy would it be to raise your son if you had some help? I want you for a second to think about an African animal. The lioness.

The female lion is the queen of the African plains. She is beautiful and strong. She is the main provider for the family, the mother, and the protector when the male is not around. Female lions are like many single women raising children in America–they suffer from the effects of lazy men. A male lion has two jobs: protect the pride from other males and procreate. That is it. They do not spend time with their kids. They are usually out looking for other lionesses to procreate with.

The female lion understands how life works without a male. Not only has she accepted this, but she has learned to bond with her female cohorts. The unit of females has become one of the strongest forces on the plains of Africa. Every other group of animals fears the pride of female lions. They are incredibly smart.

The smartest thing that these single mothers have learned to do is bond with one another from life until death. In one pride, there could be as many as three or four generations of lionesses, and they all work together to provide for their cubs– their children.

Every member of the lion pride has a specific job, from the youngest lioness to the great grandmother. They all take part in raising the cubs and finding food. Instead of fighting each other over men like some people do, the lionesses work together. Many human mothers do not want anyone else raising their kids, but working together is how the lionesses have prospered. The lionesses bond together, and I believe this approach is practical enough for human single mothers to apply.

The lioness shares everything with her sisters and relatives in the pride, even her food and living space. A female lion will even let another female's cubs suckle from her, knowing any of the other females will do the same for her children. The bond between these single mothers is the reason lionesses have succeeded in a harsh environment, even without a male's help.

If a lion can manage this in the middle of the Serengeti, what is stopping mothers from doing this in America? Maybe you do not know any other strong lionesses that you would trust with your kids? If so, this is a problem. If you do not have any strong female friends you may be hanging around the wrong people.

What else would stop you from bonding and forming a pride? Are you too *selfish* to share what you have with another woman's kids? A lot of people are too selfish to share. They try to do everything on their own. The *Lone Ranger* parenting style is not the most effective. It will only leave you worn out like the female octopus who, after rearing her young, dies and is eaten by predators. As great a single mother as the female octopus is, if the female octopus grouped with others, she would survive to see her kids grow up.

Whatever else is a barrier stopping you from building a strong group of women to raise your kids, you need to put it down. Share this thought with other mothers you know and see if they would be willing to get on board.

I recommend that not all the mothers in the group be single mothers. I strongly recommend that someone in the group have a strong marriage and a strong man at home. You do not understand how great it would be, if not only all the mothers got together to share in the parenting, but if all the young boys could have a good man to look up to and a working marriage to model. *Men learn by example–whether it is positive or negative.*

The size of the group does not matter at all. Small and large prides of lionesses thrive. The smaller prides succeed because their resources do not have to be spread so thin in order to support everyone. The larger prides succeed because there are more lions to provide resources and therefore more resources to go around.

For younger boys, your pride could hire tutors and high-quality babysitters to watch and teach your children. For older boys, your pride could also hire tutors or take turns monitoring their activities. It is up to your group what you decide to do. This thing will work if you work it with people willing to work it. Trust me. If you can love your kids at home, and then have other mothers loving them and looking out for them as if they were their own kids outside of your home, the children would be surrounded by too much attention and love to ever go wrong. If you throw in a good man or two or three to guide the boys in becoming a man, what can stop them?

Other teamwork ideas I suggest are unique. My mother actually did these things. She may not have known she was doing them, or maybe she did, but whether she did or not, they helped me to become who I am and think the way I do. My mother has always been a tough business woman. She was involved in corporate America as long as I can remember before going into entrepreneurship. Successful people surrounded her for as far back as I can remember. She would take me to work all of the time. Maybe she did this to show her boss that she had a son and needed time off to be with him, but what this did to me was give me ideas. I would walk around those big office buildings and just imagine owning one of them one day. I would sneak into people's offices, sit in their big chairs, and play talk on the office conference phones. This elevated my belief system. While I was at these buildings, I would always run into high class and important people. These people would take the time to sit down and talk to me. They would ask me what I wanted to do in the future. They would ask me all types of things. I was young, and this was way before I was drinking, doing drugs, or skipping school, so I would talk to them. At that time, I wanted to be a veterinarian. They would tell me what college I should go to, who I should talk to, and whatever else they could to help me. I would just soak up all of this knowledge. After that, they would always tell me how smart I was and how they wished they could have thought as I did when they were young.

Now that I am older, I know they were just being polite, but at the age of 8, if your mother's boss tells you they wish they could be like you, you start feeling like a somebody. As I said, my mother may not have known that she was surrounding me with success and preparing my mind for success when she took me to work with her, but I learned a lot. Every time someone took the time to talk to me, I would soak it all up, and really start to believe it. These people played an important part in my development.

I suggest bringing your son into the company of successful people. Men learn by example. Surround your children with doctors, lawyers, college-educated people, and millionaires. I remember when I met my first millionaire, and I remember sitting in offices with rich successful people that my mother was friends with. They would tell me how smart and great a thinker I was, and I would tell them things like, "One day I am going to have your job!" These experiences really shaped my thinking, and no matter how many drugs I did or how much alcohol I drank, I never lost the zeal to think big.

Surround your kids with successful people. It takes a village to raise a child.

Chapter Fifteen

Planning Ahead

Going through life without a plan is like going fishing without any bait.
— Cederick W. Tardy II

I know many of you already know how to plan, but the question is, *does your son*? Ask yourself this question: Can my son envision his future and then chart out the calculated steps he needs to take to achieve the aspiration? If you do not know for sure, this chapter is for you. This chapter focuses on planning, not for you, but for your son's future. Eighteen years is not that long.

When it was time for me to move out of my house at 18, I thought to myself, "I sure wish I had planned this better." And, you know what? I am sure my mother thought the same thing. For me, graduating high school was like missing a few stairs while walking down a staircase, and then tumbling all the way down to the floor. I realized way too late that I had made too many mistakes, and played around way too much. Since my daily routine of school and sleep was over, my mother and I had no idea what I was going to do and where I was going to go. Had we only worked as a team years ago, bonded years ago, trusted each other years ago, planned years ago, my life would have been dramatically different. Had we planned for me to go to college, planned for me to enter a technical school, or planned something for my life, we would have been much better off.

From that day on I learned: When you do not have a plan, life will offer you one free of charge. Life always gives people a plan, but those plans are usually tough for the receiver, because for the receiver they are unplanned circumstances like pregnancy, abusive relationships, or any miserable occurrence. Life gives people a destiny when they do not choose one for themselves. Why not plan then to avoid being tossed by uncertainty? If you can plan your actions, you can map out your future. It was not until I was 19, almost two years after I graduated, that I grasped the importance of planning.

Your son has his own way of thinking, and those thoughts will rarely line up with your view of what is acceptable. Your son's thoughts will line up with whatever his major influences are, whether that is BET, MTV and the like. *The only thing that can change a boy's thinking is new and better thoughts. The only thing*

Planning Ahead

that can change your son's directional course is a new and better direction. If you do not give him this direction, he will rarely find it on his own, because a teenager left up to his own policies and procedures is a tragedy in the making.

In yours son's portion of *The Connection Series, A Head Start*, I have given him a detailed chapter for planning. In it, I used an analogy of how a football game must be planned play by play, and I explained that the team with the best plan usually wins the game. I also explained that life is a war, and that no battle is ever won without a battle plan. I showed him how to brainstorm, how to organize a written plan, how to make a daily to-do list, and how to envision his plan coming to fruition. Sounds great, doesn't it? Guess what? All of this will be useless if you do not assist him in the early development stage of his life. As a child he may not be able to motivate himself.

It is your responsibility as his mother to be his coach. He does not understand the importance of repetition. Football coaches and basketball coaches do though, and that is why they produce winning teams. They practice the same plays over and over until they become *habitual*. I recommend you do the same thing for your son. Repeat the same things to him over and over and then over and over again, and enforce what you say to him.

It will take months until the principles for planning become natural to him. For example, things like making a daily to-do list will seem like a waste of time to him, but make sure he makes one daily. Have your son make a to-do list every night, and then have him show it to you before he goes to sleep. The next day, before he makes his new list, ask him how far he got on his previous list. Reward him for progress and repeat what you said the day before constantly. Instill in him the desire for planning, because planning and practice are nearest and dearest to achievement.

This chapter is not meant to degrade you, but to remind you of all the requirements needed to build a basic plan so that you can forward this information to your son repetitively. I believe that you should be highly involved in your son's planning processes. You need to assist him in thinking ahead, *now*, while he is still young, not four years down the line after he has already graduated high school. You must plan *now* how you are going to get him out of your house and onto a path toward success in life.

Left to his own devices, your son will follow a path to fun instead of stability, just as we all doubtlessly did at his age. We all thought it was more important to hang out and enjoy the freedoms of being young rather than thinking about the inevitable future of growing up. I am not trying to force you to steal your son's childhood from him by getting him to think and focus on the future. A child needs to have fun–it is crucial for his development. Playtime and hanging out have their place, but playtime and hanging out is not what gets him out of your house at 18. I have seen too many young men remain children until they are 30 years old because they were never taught to plan for their future. Planning ahead builds confidence and gives hope for the future.

Most people do not plan. Average people believe taking the time to plan is a waste of time, but successful businesses and anyone else who chooses to plan will tell you, "Time spent wisely in planning is never time wasted."

In *A Head Start*, I advised your son to plan everything! Whether it is a football play, a trip to the grocery store, his day, or what college he wants to go to and how he will get there. All of these things require planning. The level of planning is not the same, of course, for going to the store as opposed to planning for college, but the process is the same for either objective.

Whether the plan is short-term, mid-range, or long-term, your son must understand the importance of thinking the process through completely. Thinking through processes removes fear and confusion for a boy who already has so much on his mind. Your son has a lot of things on his mind that are stressful and confusing for him. These things are often trivial to you as an adult, but in his mind, they are the biggest things he has ever faced. With all these hard-hitting thoughts tumbling around in his mind, it is tough to think ahead because he is lost in the present.

Another important reason to stress the importance of planning to your son is that while he is still young and very impressionable he will come into contact with older boys, generally 18 and up, and he will want to look up to them as his male figures and role models. The bad thing is that most of these 18-year-olds will be poor role models who never planned their future and have dropped out of school to sell drugs, or are in and out of jail. That is why they are hanging out with younger kids. Your son will envision that when he is 18, he can be just like them, lazy bums who hang out all day long and chill. *Plan his future before he or someone else does.*

Remember this one statement: Your son can follow a plan with no problem, but his pride will cause him to reject a forced suggestion.

This means, if he is working with you to build the plan for his future, he will have no problems following the plan, except for the usual laziness, fear of failing, or procrastination, which are all natural for human beings. It is the forced suggestions that he cannot handle. His pride mechanism kicks in instantaneously and shuts his brain off to everything you say once you hurt his pride. No matter how good the information is you are giving, or should I say yelling at him, it will fall on deaf ears. His pride has turned you off. You will have become an enemy to his self-esteem when you attack his pride.

A forced suggestion for example is, "You are going to go to Washington State when you graduate." He may not want to go to Washington State, so you will have problems getting him to follow the plan. It is up to you whether it is worth the fight. If it is worth the fight, avoid the fight and use a different approach and appeal to help him see that your plan is better than his. Take him on a tour of Washington State, but do not force your will upon him and expect him to proceed with the plan.

Instead of forcing a plan, I recommend building a mutually acceptable plan. By doing this you will avoid triggering his pride defense mechanism. The only possible hindrances from that point on will be his fears and lack of motivation.

Remember to use wisdom when setting this plan up for him. Do not plan what you want him to do. Help him plan what he wants to do that you agree with as an appropriate and successful venture. If he wants to be a musician, do not shoot him down. Find out if he has what it takes to be a musician. If he wants to be an astronaut, do not shoot him down. Find out if he has what it takes. Never shoot down your son's dreams, unless they are going to cause him harm. Dreams are all he has. If you take those from him, he will be empty.

As you two are planning for the future you must remember that children change their minds faster than the Earth changes the weather. One week he may want to be a dentist and the next week an actor. What do you do? Rather than let him see you frustrated, I recommend that you help him get settled to a specific train of thought. If he wants to be a doctor, then start him on the track of what it takes to be a doctor. Once he changes his mind, start him on that next track. *Never get complacent and begin to ignore him and what he says he wants to be! The moment you get complacent will be the same moment he does too.*

You may start thinking, "Well I know that he will not follow through with this plan since he changes his mind so much, so isn't it a waste of time to build a plan for him that he will change his mind about next week?"

No plan is a waste of time. In fact, consider it practicing for when you do finally build that perfect plan that he will follow through until the end. You both will understand by then how to research, build a plan, and then follow through. *No plan is a bad plan except for no plan at all.* A future unplanned is awaiting unplanned events!

Below are the ten steps to building a long-term plan. Follow these steps; add your own steps, do whatever you have to do, but keep this information fresh in your son's mind.

1. Set a clear goal and write it down: This is where you will really have to understand what your son wants to do. If you are not clear on his goal, get clear. Have

him take personality tests or whatever you find applicable, but make sure you both know exactly what it is that he wants to do, and then write that goal down. Write it at the top of his plan like a title. A clear goal is the basis of a plan. When a driver's vision is clear on the road, the driver can drive at a high rate of speed to his destination, but when the driver's vision is impaired or unclear due to fog or rain, it will force the driver to slow down. Remove the fog from your son's vision by making sure he is clear on what he wants to do. He should be able to say, "I want to do or be a (Fill in the blank), by this date (Fill in the blank)."

2. Brainstorm all of your options: Write the goal on a piece of paper, draw lines off the goal, and then write down all your ideas on the lines. Brainstorming frees the mind of clutter and initial thoughts, which allows him to think more effectively towards the goal rather than trying to remember all of his ideas. Your goal as the mother will be to lend him some ideas while he is brainstorming. Use your wisdom gained over the years to assist him in his thinking process. Push him when he needs it. Keep him on track when he veers off the goal.

3. Research all of your options: Research people who have accomplished what you are facing, and get acquainted with them if possible. Research, research, research! Researching is the key to succeeding in a plan. The old adage "there is nothing new under the sun" still holds true today. Anything that your son has an inclination or interest in doing has already been accomplished and had a million books, articles, and Web pages written about it. All you two have to do is do your research.

Find those books, articles, and Web pages and start reading. Make an effort to find successful people in his field of interest that live in your area who would be willing to sit down and talk with your son. For example, when I wanted to play football my mother sent me to a football camp where I trained with Rod Woodson, and when I wanted to be a stock broker my mother sat me down with a friend of hers who was a stock broker. Research everything you can about the goal, and put together a list of options. If someone else has done it and succeeded, then in principle the same process has to work for you. Of course, you will tailor the process for your son's personality, but the basic principle stands that, "If it will work for them, it will work for him."

4. Repeat steps two and three as needed: Plans change all the time. No plan is ever set in stone and no plan should ever be thought of as unchangeable. While doing research you may find that your first ideas were way off. With that in mind you will want to re-brainstorm your ideas. Afterwards, more research may be needed.

Planning Ahead

Never attempt anything major without adequate planning. Remember that time spent planning is never time wasted. This is not to say you should wait around until you have everything you need though. You may find yourself waiting forever in that case.

5. Organize your list of options: When you are ready with all of the ideas and options you can possibly think of, you need to organize them into a list. Arrange the list by how you feel about each idea. Option number one should be what you feel the strongest about, then option two, and so on. Arranging this list gives your son a clear idea of how many different options there are to complete this goal. Remember that there is no such thing as a perfect plan, and there is no such thing as the right plan. If one option does not work, you still have a list of available options to work on. For example the list could read, "Number one – Washington State. Use the equity in home to pay for tuition. Number Two – Go to community college the first year, and build up scholarships to fund university. Number three – et cetera and so forth."

6. Begin to build your plan: Building the plan takes time. Your son should not get discouraged when planning. If it takes him a full year to build his plan, that is no problem. A big goal needs a detailed plan. Do not forget to set a deadline for the goal! A goal without a due date may never reach completion. Due dates give you a sense of urgency. The steps in the plan need to have completion dates, and the actual plan needs to have a deadline or date of achievement. You may decide to lay out the plan however you see fit.

7. Arrange the steps you need to take: Steps are important. Steps break down something as huge as a monumental vision into bite-sized chunks that are more easily swallowed. All the steps need to be broad but at the same time progressive. The steps need to be obtainable and well thought out. Set due dates for taking each step.

8. Take baby steps (daily things to do): Baby steps are simply to-do list type things. These baby steps can be daily or weekly things that he needs to do. Set due dates for taking each step.

9. Follow through: Motivation is critical. You will need to stay on his butt until he gets the hang of motivating himself. Some people may not be as motivated to succeed as others. Those less motivated people need coaches. Do not force him to succeed, but coach him to success. Remember not to push a string, but pull.

I recommend reading a book on coaching to learn valuable coaching strategies. Explain to him that a plan is useless without action. Action is what will accomplish the plan.

10. Obtain the goal: The whole purpose of making the plan and following through is to obtain the goal. It is at this point when you can rest assured–knowing you did your job as a mother. You got your son to succeed.

Never forget that you must take your son's capability to believe in himself into account. The way that your son sees the plan will determine if he will be capable of achieving it. If he thinks it is going to be too hard, then it will be too hard for him. If he can see the plan as something uncomplicated, something that he only has to follow through with to reach the end prize, then he will be all set mentally for success. The way he sees the plan will determine if he will be capable of achieving it. Don't make the plan frightening or dreadful.

Along with this I recommend that before you try to build a long-range plan for your son, build some smaller plans that may only take two to three days to accomplish. These plans should have few steps and few to-do's. Consider them practice. Get your son used to the process. Accomplishing these small plans will boost his confidence in his ability to follow a plan. Once he can accomplish a week-long plan, then bump him up to a month-long plan and so on. Remember that if he is confident he will see the plan, no matter how long, as obtainable, and then he will be able to achieve the end result.

Good luck on your future endeavors, and if you have any questions, send me a letter or an e-mail. (See page 159 for complete contact information.)

Chapter Sixteen

The Power of God's Word

Without faith in something bigger than ourselves–without something else holding us up–we will crumble when the weight of the world is placed on our shoulders.
— Cederick W. Tardy II

As a Christian, I felt it was utterly important for me to include this chapter. I believe in my heart that these books are a part of the reason I was placed on this Earth, and by my completion of them, I am fulfilling my purpose here. This chapter is in no way an attempt to force my spiritual beliefs upon anyone. This chapter is simply a suggestion that I believe will help someone. I would be robbing that person if I did not add this chapter to this book. If you are not a Christian, if you do not want any of your family to be Christian, if you are against the Word of Jesus, Jehovah, God, the Bible, or any word of faith or church, then I would recommend that you go on to the next chapter. But, just know that nothing–*absolutely nothing*–got my family out of our living hell except the Word of God.

I want the mothers who are open to receiving the truth to know that a major component of my transformation was the fact that I began hooking up with the Word of the Bible. If you do not currently go to church but always thought it might do some good, or if you do go to church but do not see any change, or if you have never thought about church but are interested in what I have to say about this matter, then I recommend you keep reading. This just may be what you needed to read.

When I was in the 10th grade, I was really getting into the party scene. I smoked a lot of weed and drank as much as I could. I would go out every weekend, and I even treated the weekdays as party nights. I can remember one day my mother telling me to get dressed in something nice because we were going to church. "Church?" I asked. "Yes, we are going to church." Until then, I do not think I had ever gone to an actual church. I remember walking into church thinking about how boring it was going to be. My initial thoughts were wrong though. I actually liked what I heard that night.

Liking what I heard did not matter much though. I still smoked weed the next day and went on about my life as normal, but something was different. After going to church, instead of just running around freely, it felt like I had finally gained a conscience. You know, that little guy in your ear who tells you what is right and wrong? That guy had finally been awakened. I did my best to ignore him, but the more and more my mother kept bringing me to church, the louder and louder he got. I felt bad that I would go to church regularly and still do drugs–and sell them. I can remember many times trying to quit smoking, but I never could quite do it. The good thing was that even though I was still doing the drugs, at least I wanted to quit, which is step number one.

During that first year of going to church regularly, I ended up going to a big teen extravaganza. The church put on a four-day event that was strictly for teenagers. The ministers there were reformed drug dealers, gangsters, and thugs and they spoke to the crowd of 3500 as real as they were allowed to in a church building. I can remember seeing teens weeping and crying at the altar who otherwise looked like they could shoot you at any second. I can remember that is when I was given the passion to write for the benefit of others. This passion was burned in to me that night.

As I sat in the church listening to the minister, he asked any teen in the crowd who felt that they had a purpose in their life to raise their hand. I raised my hand because I always felt like I was special. He asked everyone who raised their hands to come to the front. I walked up to the front of the room, and immediately the minister started touching people and speaking over people. A little surprised at what I was seeing, I stayed there. The man walked up to me, touched my head and asked me what I was good at. I said, "I love to write poetry," and he replied, "One day your writings will be used to help young people all over America and the world."

I went back to my seat a little shook up. I was trying to figure out how my poetry would someday help the mass of teens I saw in front of me. Remember, my poetry was so dark and depressing that my mother had to get me a psychiatrist.

Let me rewind my life back to before 10th grade. At the age when I could finally grasp a little of what was going on, I was very interested in the Bible and what it had to say. After hearing about it, it was like a fear of God and hell had been placed in my heart. This fear is what this chapter is about, because I believe this fear is what kept me out of a lot of trouble and what ultimately changed my life.

No matter how rough my life got or how bad I ever was, I was always scared of going to hell and abided by a lot of morals, unlike many people I knew without a Christian background. Hearing the message of torment and hell as a little kid frightened me, and that fear stuck with me. I know for sure I would not have come around as quickly as I did without the Word.

I was never comfortable stealing, lying, or doing a lot of things once that little man, my conscience, was awakened inside of me. He would tug on my heart every time. Like many people, I was a sinner who whenever he got in trouble would always cry out to God. The difference though was that I really wanted something better for my life–I just never knew how to get it. Your boy may be the same way. Nobody really wants to be stuck in the mud. Everyone would rather be free.

I never wanted to do wrong, but slowly over those years as other influences came into my life, my heart grew cold and my mother had a real problem on her hands. Then in 10th grade she got me to the therapist, better yet, she got me to church. The reverential fear I had of God, hell, and satan was like a long rope. No matter how far out I got, He was able to pull me back by that rope. I never wanted to spend eternity in torment.

Mothers, please pay attention to this. I was about 15 years old when my mother started bringing me to church regularly. On the outside, I hated going to church. I would put up a big fight sometimes. I would go to church stoned (really high) sometimes, trying to make her not take me, and then I would get there and pretend that I was not listening. I would go as far as to make crazy faces at the preacher while he was teaching to try and mess him up.

My mother could have saved herself plenty of embarrassment and just quit taking me to church, but she knew what she had to do. She understood that if I heard anything repeatedly it would have an affect on me, just like the rap music I was listening to all day, every day. I would sit in church and pretend I hated it there so much, but all the while, I was listening. I was always fascinated by the Bible's impact on the world. Things did not change overnight though. My mother knew that I was going to go home right after church, fire up a blunt, and zone out like I did every day, but she kept taking me to church at least twice a week.

I yearned for God, but I was so addicted to smoking weed I could not let it go. Week after week, I would listen to the preacher talk, and I even started to remember some of the scriptures I heard regularly. The first scripture I ever remembered was *Job 36:11*, which reads, "If they obey and serve him they will spend their days in prosperity and their years in pleasure." The best part was that I could see that scripture every time I looked at my pastor. Seeing him living prosperously excited me because I saw an authoritative and rich black man who was not a rapper, pimp, or drug dealer. Gradually I began to turn. I was still acting a fool every weekend, but cutting back more and more.

To make a long story a shorter one, three years after that first day in church, I was volunteering in the church, using my writing to help teens. I was a volunteer writer for one of the church's teen-directed television programs. I used some of my real-life experiences to inform adults of what a teen in this generation was going through. I decided to stop smoking weed, I signed up for the Navy, and a few months later, I shipped off. I was out of my hometown and away from those negative influences. Granted, my first couple years in the Navy were a partial relapse back into what I had just escaped, but I smartened up, got back into church, and things will never relapse again.

The Bible, when understood, plants a reverential fear in the heart of a person and that fear affects the conscience. The Word of God will only have an affect on your son when heard repetitiously, read regularly, understood, and embraced as the truth. The change that will take place will be gradual, and that is what you must remember. You cannot take your boy to church once or twice and think that he is going to clean himself up and never do anything wrong again. My total transformation has been a five and a half year process just to get to where I am now, and I am far from faultless. I slipped up many times during those years, and if you did not know me, you probably would not have known I loved God and was trying my best to be a Christian. I had to be saved over and over again until I finally felt saved. I coined this type of person with the phrase "habitual salvation receiver." I was scared to go to hell.

My advice to you, mom, is that you get your son into church as soon as possible. Get him into a church that he likes and can respect. Not every church is the same. Had my pastor not been such a commanding man I would not have believed what he was saying. Now that I am older I know that the pastor is not what matters, and that the Word is what matters, but to a new Christian the church and pastor have to be right.

Take your son to church every time the doors are open. The more he is at church, the less time he is out in the streets. And, if you can afford to, take him out to eat every time after you go to church. Make going to church a regular family outing. My mother used to take me out to eat after church sometimes. Even when I did not want to go to church, I knew I was going to eat some good food afterwards, so I would go anyway.

I also recommend buying your son a Bible, but not just any Bible. Get him a Today's English Version Bible. Why? For me, and for many other people I am sure, reading the King James Version Bible is difficult. I read the King James Version of the Bible for years and never truly grasped it. Then one day I picked up the Today's English Version and everything I had read for years finally made sense. The English reads a lot easier, and that is a plus for a new Christian.

If possible, mom, do what my mother never did with me–read the Bible with your son. My mother was learning the Word about the same time I was, so maybe she was not comfortable sitting down and reading the Bible with me, but I believe that it would have made a huge difference in our relationship to share something like that. Try reading the Bible with him once a week or so to begin with. Also, be sure not to bash him over the head with the Bible and the Word. I have watched many men have their pride hurt and never come back to God because some Christian tried to beat them over the head with the Bible. It is not your job to scare your boy into submission. The Word will do all of that on its own. You will only repel him if you are always in his face talking about Jesus this, and Jesus that.

Also, be sure that you explain to your child that there will always be hypocrites in the church. Do this early on and make sure he understands that not everyone in church is doing the right thing, and that not everyone at church is necessarily a hypocrite. Explain that most church people are in a stage of transformation themselves. They may just be beginning to change their ways and therefore the way you see them now is not how they will always be. Be sure to explain all of this, because a new Christian can often be repelled and offended by church hypocrites. Be sure that you yourself are not one of the church hypocrites! Your son will be watching your every move closely to find out if this is real or not. Make sure you explain to him before you send him to any of the teenager parts of the church that not all of the kids are there for the right reasons. Many of the boys and girls there are just there to hook up. He needs to know not to hook up with the wrong church crowd because they will get him in trouble just like the wrong school crowd will.

The difference in my life and behavior now from five and a half years ago is farther apart than black and white. My family and my mother know where my life would be if I had not gotten into church. Church, for me, was like a seatbelt or an air bag in a car accident. I wrecked my life plenty of times, but the safety features were already built in, and for that reason I was fortunate to be able to walk away from a mangled life with only minor scars and injuries.

The Bible has power. The power comes from the reverence that it places in the heart of a person after they accept the message. Remember the transformation will be gradual, but the change will come.

Chapter Seventeen

Do You Put Off Until Tomorrow What Should Have Been Done Yesterday?

When making a promise, make it good. When telling a lie, stop yourself.
— Cederick W. Tardy II

This chapter is about parental procrastination. If unchecked, parental procrastination can and will do some severe damage to the bond between mother and son. This is not a bash-my-mother session, or bash-you-mothers session, but it is an honest attempt to expose some ideas about your actions as a mother and the way your son interprets them.

Have you ever told your son that you would do something, but you never did it? This is a vicious cycle that starts at the top and tears a wedge all the way down the love line.

Has your boss ever offered you a favor, and then reneged on the offer? Does it upset you when a relative is supposed to bring something of yours by the house, but never shows? What about the dreaded repairman or cable guy who makes you wait for two days before he actually arrives at your house? Aren't these irritating instances? And don't they make you never want to use their services again? Why would your child not feel any different if you tell him that you will do something, but you never do? The excuses you give him are never more valid than the promise you made.

There are two main points in this chapter. First, I want to get across the importance of communication on a daily basis about your life. If your child is clueless about your schedule and the demands placed on your shoulders as a single mother, then how can you expect him to be compassionate about them? You have to do more than tell him what you are going through; you have to make sure he understands it. Walk him through a day of your life until he gets it. Secondly, I want to get across the idea that if you say you are going to do something, you must do it to save your mother-son relationship.

Do you put off until tomorrow what should have been done today? Procrastination is normal human behavior, but that does not make it acceptable.

PUTTING IT OFF

Do What You Said You Would

Do what you say you are going to do when you said you were going to do it. This is the most important non-essential parental responsibility there is between parent and child. I say non-essential only because I think food, water, and shelter are the essentials, and then after that come love, trust, patience, and respect. As a single mother you have a multitude of duties, but keeping your word is a big one. Without keeping your word on a consistent basis, distrust and enmity will settle in and drive a wedge between you and your son that only time apart will heal.

As a mother, the head of the household, the sole role model, you should not go around making and breaking your promises.

What happens if you take out a loan for a car, and then you never pay on that car? The company will come and repossess that car, won't they? Not only that, but you will build a bad credit reputation. This bad credit reputation basically says about you, "I am not trustworthy, my word means nothing, and I am very irresponsible."

Take the credit principle and apply it to parenting. A promise not kept is likened to a demand for payment not paid. It is your responsibility to repair your credit with those credit companies, and if you have broken your trust with your son, then you need to set up a plan to build your credit back with your son. Start small. You can do things like, buy a pair of basketball tickets way in advance, tell your boss your plan, and then a week before the game tell your son you are taking him to the game. You already have the tickets, so that can't fail. Your boss already knows you need to build a better mother-son relationship to keep your relationship intact, so he or she shouldn't bother you. All you have to do now is take him to the game.

Since you have planned ahead and eliminated almost every chance of failure, you are almost guaranteed to get to the game. Even if you have to check the car battery in advance, check traffic, and go in early to work that day, do what you have to do to get on the right track. I guarantee if you make it to that game that night, a little switch will click in your son's head.

When you tell your son a week in advance that you two are going to do something, he will not even listen to you if you have been untrustworthy in the past. Your words will go in one ear and out the other. It will be your responsibility to reinforce to him daily, hourly, bi-hourly, to make sure he is ready to go to the game next week (or whatever you decide to do with him). Not only will the reinforcement help him remember, but it will also help you remember!

Once that next week comes around, and the two of you are in the car with your team jerseys on, on your way to the game, he will be looking at you differently, believe me. Wondering, "Is this real?" "Is she actually doing what she said?" "This must be a one-time thing." Whatever he is thinking, he will just be glad to see you finally do what you said you were going to do. Things like this really work.

That example was good and helpful if you already have damaged your credibility with your son, but what if you haven't yet? Maybe your son is just too young and can't really tell the difference. Your job is simple. You do not have to do all sorts of damage repair. Your job is damage prevention. Simply do what you say you are going to do at all times. And if you do not think you will be able to do something, then do not say you will. If you have already said you will, but things change so much that you have to renege then make sure you apologize and fully explain. It is really that easy to keep the trouble out–do not give trouble an opportunity to come in.

If your son asks you to take him somewhere or buy him something, and you do not know if you will be able to, do not say maybe, because maybe is closer to yes than no. Instead, say "NO" until you know for sure if there will be a yes or a no. It will always be better for you to say "no" first, then an hour later take him where he wants to go, than to say "yes," and an hour later have to say "no."

Keep your credibility as a parent if you want your son to trust you, listen to you and respect you without having to yell or threaten.

Communication

My mother and I, thank God, finally came to amends. Before we hardly spoke. If we did, she was telling me stuff I didn't want to hear, and I was telling her stuff a child should never tell his mother. The relationship is now wonderful. I come to her with questions and she comes to me with questions, and the answers go both up and down, side to side. This type of relationship was possible years ago, and that is what hurts the most. I know a lot of the pain was my fault, but I cannot assume all of the blame. We were in this mother-and-son thing together.

What was the problem? Our problem was that we never spoke. And if we did speak, all I heard was negative stuff that really turned me off, and all she heard was my smart-aleck remarks. Instead of my strong tower and support system, like a mother should be, she was more like my emotional bulldozer and I was the same to her. This type of relationship, brought on by a lack of positive communication, led me to look for other means of acceptance.

The key is to talk to your son way before the situation gets as bad as the relationship between my mother and I was. Once the situation gets to a point where it seems like there is no return, there really may be no road of return. That bridge may not be there anymore if it has been burned and busted up by lies, hurting, and emo-

Putting It Off

tional soreness.

Do not put communication off until tomorrow that you know your child needs today. I suggest setting up a schedule, an allotted time schedule, just for your son. Allot him as much time as you can and then gradually find ways to implement more time. This will take away time from your personal life, but remember this, your son never asked to come to your house. It would be rude to invite a guest over and not spend any time with them.

Studies show that an active and stimulating environment is important for healthy brain development. Make sure you keep your conversations active and enjoyable. You cannot torture the poor boy by sitting him down in the living room, staring at him, and telling him how you feel. Instead be exciting. Make it like a date! Take him out for ice cream, root beer floats, or something you know he would enjoy. Be sure that it is just the two of you. You cannot have a meaningful conversation at a football or basketball game. Take him out fishing, even if you do not like to or know how to fish. Events like these give plenty of time for good wholesome laughing and conversation. You never know what you might learn from a child who is willing to express himself.

This is important, so I will emphasize it once again. Make your hang out activities with your son fun. Make them exciting. I recommend taking the time to do things you never thought of. Even if you do not have the money to go to the movies, shopping, or to get ice cream, you can go for walks in different areas of town. You could go house hunting, even if you know you can't afford the house. Both of you can get dressed up and go look at a million dollar home or two one weekend. Things like these will give you not only something to laugh about, but you will have ample time to communicate while driving. Remember these are just some suggestions; you are open to do anything, but just be sure to do something.

A little side bar that concerns conversation in the car; the radio should be on at a minimum. How can you converse properly if you have music playing? If you are not used to talking to your son, then music can be appropriate, but in moderate amounts. And one last tidbit: Even if you do not like the music that he listens to, put that station on anyway. Remember, his music is saying what he really wants to. This gives you a chance to listen to him speak to you without him even knowing he is doing so.

You would never tell your fiancé you will get back to him about the date of marriage. You would never tell your boss you do not have time to do what you said you would do. So why would you ever do things similar to that to your own son? If it would hurt you, then it is going to hurt him, and probably more so because he is younger and may not be able to cope with his emotions yet.

Chapter Eighteen

Just Some Thoughts

If kids have no concept of reality, it is not because of video games, music or TV. It is because no one has shown them what reality really is.
—Cederick W. Tardy II

When I was growing up, my mother was always very busy. She sometimes had to work two jobs just to keep our heads above water. Granted she did spend a lot of her money on junk and doodads, but for the most part, she did her best to put food on the table and a roof over my head. I respect her for the hard work and time she sacrificed to keep me healthy. I only resent the fact that she was not around when I needed her. When I needed someone to talk to, she was at work. My dad never gave me any real advice. My grandmother, bless her heart, tried her best.

Most of the time I would just think to myself about my problems. When you talk to someone, you get your problems off your chest, but when you talk to yourself, your problems just stay with you. I ended up really going crazy inside of my head because I had no one to talk with. I tried talking to my friends, but they could not understand what I was feeling; they were just kids like me. If they did understand how I felt, it was only because they were going through the same thing. Instead of getting advice or consolation for my problems, I would be bombarded with a friend's problems as well as mine. We would end up getting so depressed we would just find something to get us high to forget the problems.

Mothers, I want you to think about whether it's possible that you do not spend enough time with your kids, especially your teenagers. Does your son come to you with questions looking for advice? Yes, or no?

If yes, are you able to help him adequately with his problems? If you can answer yes to both of these questions then I salute you, but to the mothers who answered no to both, keep reading.

One problem we have to deal with is why your child does not come to you for advice. You know he has to have problems going on in life; everyone has problems. What is the barrier between him and you?

Just Some Thoughts

The barrier is that he may not trust you for guidance, instruction, and wisdom. Additionally, he may not believe that you will listen. Maybe in the past you have been very critical of him. Instead of coming to you with problems he will try to hide them from you to avoid your harsh criticism. You will build trust with your son when he knows and believes that you love him and are not his worst enemy. Moms, whether you believe it or not, your son just wants you to truly love him. Your son wants you to pick him up and hug and kiss him and tell him you love him. That is what a child needs. He just does not want you doing it in public.

So many parents stop hugging and kissing their boys too early. The stereotype is that this will make them sissies and punks. The stereotype is boys are supposed to be strong and tough. Problem? Think about the image you would like for your husband. You want him to be loving and caring, right? How do you expect him to be loving and caring if he does not learn that at a young age? He cannot.

Men, bound by the masculine stereotype, have been taught to be hard, tough, and rigid. That is who they try to be, and when they get older their wife expects them to be loving and caring, but they cannot do that. Loving and caring while being hard and rigid is an oxymoron. The key is to start him off young. Help his future wife out. Never stop loving your boy. Never stop kissing him and telling him you love him. He wants you to. I do not care if he carries a gun and sells drugs, wake him up in the morning and kiss him. Tell him by your words and actions that you are still his mother and that you still love him. It is crucial, believe me. Every boy wants his mother to love him.

I believe this behavior on your part, mothers, will cause these young boys to start treating women better in their future. They will treat them as women, like their mother, instead of as objects. This is just my opinion. Just some thoughts. Remember that change is gradual, so if he does not change his behavior now, he will change later simply because he will remember how much you loved him and wanted better for him. One day it will all come together for him. That day may not be tomorrow but it will be someday, and really that is all that we have. We have someday, some day in the future. That is the day that we can hope for change.

Your boy won't change because the two of you read a book. He will change because of an inward desire to change. The books are merely an eye opener to the possibilities, but only he can walk the road he chooses. *Your job is to keep that road clean and the path to it clear.* Remind him of that road every day, but do it only with love and affection. As sure as the sun will rise tomorrow, if you try to force him down a better path, he will push off of you and run speedily toward a worse path.

Chapter Nineteen

Stop Fighting With Your Son and Teach Him

You can yell at an untrained dog until you are blue in the face in an attempt to make him sit, but he will not sit. Train him how to sit, and he will sit whenever you tell him.
- Cederick W. Tardy II

"Why would I take advice from such a monster? Why should I listen to this crazy woman? Who does she think she is? She makes mistakes too!" These are the thoughts of a boy who gets nagged at all the time.

A huge mistake that mothers make when dealing with their irrational teenager is consistently pointing out every negative thing he does wrong. Like a heat seeking missile tracks on to a jet, it seems that is how parents seek the negatives of their child's life.

I am not telling you to act like there is nothing wrong, or to avoid confrontation. What I am saying is, if your way of confronting your son is not working, you really need to try a new tactic. Pointing out negatives only brings strife and causes your son anger. *If the only things your son can remember when you are around are bad times, then he will subconsciously begin to resent you.* Just the mere thought of you being around him will repulse him. He will become allergic to you and to your negative attitude.

Your son is a man, just like any other man in the world. He has the same character traits as every other man in the world. What is one thing men really hate? Nagging. What has happened every time you have nagged or yelled at a man in your life? He walked away from you, maybe said some harsh things, and began to resent you. Men get upset when a woman is always pointing out their flaws. Your son is no different than any other man. Just as a grown man cannot stand nagging, your son is going to hate the fact you are always complaining and nagging about his actions. His misbehavior and smart remarks are signs of his frustration.

Every time you pointed out a mistake that a boyfriend made in a relationship, what happened? He got upset. Right? He probably said some harsh things, stormed out, and the relationship was tarnished. Right? Why would your son, a young man, act any differently?

"He should act differently because I am his mother and he needs to respect me!" you may say. It is true he should respect you as his mother, but the reality is that this unquestionable respect may not happen until he has grown up and can come to appreciate your sacrifices.

If you are nagging at your son, he is going to get mad at you just like every other man in your life got mad at you. If you are okay with him being mad at you then stop reading this book. However, if you want to help your child adjust to life and set him up for success, then please take these recommendations to heart. *Remember, your words of instruction will never get past his barriers of mistrust and resentment. If your son doesn't like you, he is not going to listen to you, at all.*

Would you hang around someone or take advice from someone who is always saying, "You messed up on this. You did this wrong. Why did you do this? Who told you to do that?" Are you going to want that person at your birthday party? Or, will you do your best to disassociate yourself from that individual? A young boy will do the same thing to his nagging mother. He will become allergic to your nagging. The best medicine for this allergy is sound advice. Nagging solves nothing, but advice cures headaches for years to come.

Stop picking fights with your son. You must stop arguing first. Express yourself without arguing. You only look like a kid if you are starting arguments with him. As soon as the argument is over all he is thinking about is how you need to grow up and act like an adult. So, act like an adult. Control the conversation. Refrain from threats, physical abuse, yelling, cursing, and throwing a fit. Control yourself and the swing of events.

A good approach to use on a man to get your point across without rubbing him the wrong way is to use stories. Tell stories that subtly emphasize the point you wish to make instead of coming straightforward with your request. The difference in this approach is as big as the difference between Kool-Aid with and without sugar. *It is so much easier to swallow when sweetened.*

Here is an example that took place right around the time I wrote this chapter. My friend, whom I take to church regularly, does not participate in praise and worship. While everyone else sings and claps along, he stands there. So instead of saying, "You need to sing and clap like everyone else." I used the subtle approach. I snuck it in on him and he had no idea I was even referring to him. After church, I told him about when I first started going to church and would stand around while everyone was singing. I told him how I didn't think it was important to praise like everyone else. Then I told him a funny story about an older lady standing next to me one day who completely embarrassed me when she asked me why I was not singing and clapping. I told my friend how upset I was with her at first, but now, after what she said, I sing, clap, and enjoy it.

THE BIG PAYBACK

After I explained this story to him, we went to church another day. I saw the woman walking into the church so I pointed her out to make sure he hadn't forgotten what I said. The story was registering in his brain. He was thinking about how he doesn't clap, and how he just stands there. As we walked into the church I was still laughing about how silly I used to be for not clapping and singing, and that now I realize how important it is. When the music came on I glanced at him, and to no surprise at all, he was two-stepping, clapping, and singing along.

I didn't point him out. I didn't nag. I didn't embarrass him like the lady did to me–even though her method worked too. All I did was tell him a story about how important it was to praise in church, and he got the message through the story. This approach works on men. Subtly give your son a picture of what you expect without pointing at him and he will pick this up as what you expect of him without you ever referring to him.

I also recommend that you try to change the subject when things get heated. Don't ignore or beat around a heated subject, just change it. You need to control the conversation. If he gets mad, do not let him stay mad, quickly change the subject.

"This is the worst advice ever, Cederick! What do you mean change the subject? Change the subject to what? Sports?" you may be thinking.

No, my friends, you do not change the subject to sports or the day's events. You need to change the subject from an intense argument to a *counsel session*. Does this suggestion sound as if it might make some sense? Think about it. He is yelling and you are yelling. You are both acting like children. Instead, you switch the game on him. You show up to the game with some wisdom, and control the conversation from that moment on. You do not raise your voice. You raise your intellectual level a few notches.

You have to keep in mind that the conflict-causing situation has passed already. It is not time to pull his teeth out. It is time to focus on preventing the incident from happening ever again. If your son happens to get suspended from school for fighting, you do not need to whip his butt, the situation has passed already–you can whip if that is what you desire to do. After you whip him though, you need to educate him. A whipping is ineffective by itself. You need to sit him down and figure out what made the situation get to the point of a fight, and then help him learn different ways to resolve the matter without a physical altercation if possible. Nagging solves nothing. *Solutions solve problems.*

Advice given to a preteenager or teenager has to be solid, understandable, and repeated on a continual basis. Do not say to your son, "Look, boy, I told you a hundred times already!" This will only turn him off. Say instead, "Son, do you remember what I said during our talk?" Let him answer the question with a straight answer. Don't take "uh huh" or "I don't know" or shoulder shrugging for an answer. Lead him into the conversation. Lead him in with questions that take more than one word to answer.

Another subject changer I recommend is randomly quoting phrases of wisdom. If you and your son are arguing while you are cooking, just say something profoundly intelligent, and then go back to cooking. Why would you do this? Because he will be shocked. What you said will have been so out of the ordinary to him that he has no choice but to hear it. He has no choice but to think about what you said. This technique is like hiding behind a wall, and then as your friend walks by you jump out and scare her. She will have no choice but to be shocked because the deed was so random. Your random advice will ring long in his ears–even longer then your yelling.

This random-advice technique will also open the door for a meaningful conversation, because he will have to make a reply. If you need a clue about what to say randomly, I suggest short quotes, or just whatever piece of advice you think will help him. Tell him, "A quitter never wins." Then just be quiet and let that soak in. He will turn around and say, "What?" Just repeat it again, "A quitter never wins." He will most likely think about it, and just walk away. Then you can sit back and laugh about it, and he will go to his room thinking, "A quitter never wins? A quitter never wins?" I put money on it that within the next day or two he will repeat whatever random advice you gave him to his group of friends in an attempt to sound educated.

Keep in mind that you can only tell your son what you know. If what you know has gotten you nowhere or not where you want your son to be at your age, then you need to teach your kid something better or he will end up where you are. With education comes opportunity.

Stay on top of your education to educate your son. If you are no smarter than your son, why should he listen to you? That would be like a 16-year-old, first-time driver taking driving lessons from another 16-year-old, first-time driver. Both of them will end up with that car in a ditch if they do not learn something outside of what they know about driving.

The more knowledge you obtain, the more knowledge you can give out at those random times. Becoming a life-long learner will help you:
1. Obtain more tools for success
2. Help your son benefit from your knowledge
3. Set an example and become your son's advice counselor

My mother reading a book was just as good as reading the book myself. If she learned something I learned something, because she would tell me about it.

Whenever my mother learned something, she passed down the knowledge to me. When I was young I didn't want to hear any of it. Why did I not listen to my mother when I was sober and young?

The answer comes from the beginning of this chapter. She was always nagging! This nagging led to my resentment and allergy to her presence, and that allergic reaction to her became the barrier that prevented me from hearing anything she had to say. I ignored everything she had to say when I was age 13 to 19, because from age zero to 13, all she did was spank me, yell at me, curse at me, and so on.

"Why would I take advice from such a monster? Why should I listen to this crazy woman? Who does she think she is? She makes mistakes too!" These are the types of thoughts kids who get nagged at all the time have.

I did not trust my mother from age 13 to 19, because of the resentment I had built toward her from zero to 13. I felt like she was a bully, and no one willingly complies to a bully unless they are a wimp. I was no wimp, and neither is your son. He is a young man, proud, and hardheaded. For him to be led by anyone, the leader must portray qualities of distinguished character and sound judgment.

Once my mother began to incorporate the character traits into her life that I expected from a parent, I was able to follow her example of continuing my education, reading vast numbers of books, networking with people, and starting a business. The key was not how much advice she gave me, but how much of it I was willing to accept as truth from her. She needed me to trust her before I would trust her words. She had to quit spanking me, yelling at me, cursing, drinking, contradicting herself, and treating me like a second rate citizen to build the trust that she desired and I needed.

How do some of these suggestions sound compared to what you have been trying? You can keep spanking and/or yelling if you wish, but there will come a day when your son will no longer be physically scared of you anymore. That is when you had better know how to hold influence over him without the use of fear. Do not ignore discipline. Try new approaches at disciplining. The old parenting style of soap in the mouth, slaps, pops, and switches is outdated. *Education is the key.*

Education is the key to a better life. This is not to say that education guarantees success, but education does open up more doors and opportunities. Educating your son ensures that he will be able to cope with the real world. The more *Real Life 101* lessons he has on his transcript, the easier his transit out of the home will be.

Speak nothing but good things to your child to receive good things in return. Parents are always telling their kids what they cannot do. "Boy, you can't do this. Boy, you cannot do that." Instead, try telling him what he can do. You already know from your experiences as a child that whatever your mother told you not to do, you wanted to do even more. Try telling him what he can do, and just watch what happens.

"Boy, you can be a dentist" or "I can see you being a songwriter." Tell him things like this as you drive around the city. "Son, I can see you working in a high rise one day, at the top floor. CEO." It can't hurt him if you say these things. He may not believe you, but at least he isn't hearing you say, "What happened at school today? How come you didn't take out the trash? Why didn't you wash the dog? Do you hate me? What's wrong? And so forth."

Tell him about all of the vast opportunities there are for him in life. As a child, he is not able to see far beyond this present day. He cannot see beyond what his hands can reach. You have to be his eyes and ears until he becomes an adult. What I mean is, you will have to point out opportunities to him until he is able to see them for himself. Animal parents do this all of the time. The mother animal takes her child out into the forest and shows her baby what is good to eat, what their predators look like, and when and where to look for food and shelter. You will have to see opportunities for your son, and you will have to articulate them to him as animal mothers do for their children. I always used to say, "How can you expect me to do what I have never been taught or told about?"

A lot of parents make the mistake of telling their kids where they cannot hang out in the city that they live in. Try telling him where he can hang out. Kids are always complaining about having nothing to do, and that is because no one is showing them what to do. Instead, they are using their imaginations. The things they are imagining are school shootings, blowing stuff up, robbing people, car chases, and so forth. Take the time to tell him about his city. Tell him about the city's history, and show him the best places around the town. My mother used to tell me a lot about the city of Houston, and what happened is I grew to respect my city. I didn't want to litter there. I didn't want to paint graffiti. I had a respect for the city because it became personal. Let your son know about the better things to do in town, and you will stop hearing, "I am bored."

No man, no matter what age, wants to be yelled at. No man, no matter what age, wants to be yelled at by a woman especially. No man, no matter what age, wants to hear a woman nagging about small details or even big details. No man wants to hear a women constantly telling him what he did wrong for the day. He will distance himself from you as far and as much as possible until he becomes allergic to you.

Stop picking fights with your son and just teach him. If the parent can learn how to deal with the kid with a positive attitude, and the kid can focus on something better than partying, drugs, and girls, you will both benefit.

Chapter Twenty

Suicide

The best way to save a friend's life is to help make his life worth living; make him feel needed.

- Cederick W. Tardy II

The suicide rate among black male teenagers has more than doubled, and has now become the third leading cause of death among black male teenagers. According to the Centers for Disease Control, in 1980, the suicide rate among whites ages 10 to 19 was 157 percent greater than that of blacks of the same age group. However, by 1995 there was only a 42 percent difference. This is not a racial issue at all. In my opinion, *we* as a *human* race have a problem, and the problem is not specific to one color.

I thought long and hard about adding this chapter before I actually did it. This was one of the hardest chapters for me to write. Partly because I did not know much about suicide, and partly because I did not want to scare any parents into thinking that their son was suicidal. The fact is, suicide is real and serious; it is real serious. My intent is not to reiterate things said in the past by psychiatrists. I wish to share my side of the suicide story, and perhaps give you insight into suicide among young males in this generation. Please remember I am not trying to and cannot speak for every young man on this aspect, but I want to inform those who are unaware that suicide among black teenage males is a prevalent dilemma.

My Own Suicide Story

Let me tell the story of how I tried to commit suicide and then I will shine light as to why I let it go that far.

Believe it or not, I tried to commit suicide at a small party surrounded by my friends. I was not in a corner crying about how bad life was, and I was not sitting on the couch with a pistol in my mouth. I was 17 years old, in 12th grade, and living what some would consider an exciting life. I had a car, money, friends, parties to go to, and everything else. At this party I was smoking, drinking, and hanging out with my friends. That is when one of them decided he wanted to go to the

SUICIDE

garage and show us what was in there.

As we all looked around the garage, we saw tanks and tanks full of Freon, which is the gas used in refrigerators and air conditioners. His father worked for an air conditioning company. Previously on television we had watched a group of teenagers take the gas, empty it into trash bags, and inhale the gas. The light bulb went off in all of our heads, and my friend ran to grab a few trash bags.

With trash bags in hand, we figured out how to get the gas into the bags without freezing ourselves and argued with each other about who would go first. This type of high lasts only for about 10 to 60 seconds, but it is free. You can also get this type of high by inhaling the fumes from a whipped cream canister, a can of Computer Keyboard Duster, or from a single-shot CO_2 canister into a balloon. The street name for this high is called a "whip it" nationwide.

Since it was my friend's house and his idea, he decided to go first. Two puffs later, I watched him violently jolt and then hit the floor in a giggling and convulsing sort of fit. Then he passed out. The rest of us watched as he twitched a little. About 20 seconds later, he woke up and shook the high off. He said it was funny. We were already drunk and high so we all decided to try it. One by one, we were dropping like flies and giggling like hyenas. My first time was like nothing I had ever experienced, and like nothing I could explain in writing. It was fun enough to decide to do again, even though we knew how horrible it was for our brains. This, parents, is a condition called "slow suicide," which I will talk more about later.

After we had our fill, everyone went back into the living room to let our heads level back out. About two hours later we decided to do it again. This time we were going to see who could huff the most before passing out. When my turn came around, I huffed a full trash bag, and then decided to go for another one. As the oxygen was depleting from my brain I thought to myself, "If I do any more there is a chance I might die." I huffed it again, fell down with the bag in hand, and then took another huff. Another huff and another one while on the ground, the room was disappearing and my only thoughts were, "It would probably be all right if I did not wake back up from this. After all, at least I'm going out having fun. Everyone will remember me too. It might be cool. I wonder what is on the other side when you die."

I went for another huff and then everything turned black. A few moments later, I opened my eyes again to see my friends standing around me laughing about how much Freon I had huffed. Disappointed that I woke back up, I laughed along with the crowd, and lay there a while to gather my bearings. It took a while to hit me, but I had actually tried to take myself out. When I got back up, I decided then and there never to do that again–huff Freon or try to kill myself.

So what happened to make me try to kill myself anyway–in this way, in this

116

setting, at this time in my life?

Honestly, I do not know to this day. I guess I had always been fascinated with the idea of ending the mental anguish caused by the pressures of life. I wanted to get away from home, I wanted to meet God to ask him a few questions, I wanted to meet Satan to ask him what his problem was, and I wanted to get away from where I was. Most of all I was scared of my future with the way I was living at the present. All of those thoughts, mixed with drugs and alcohol, fueled my anguish and before I knew it, I was trying to eradicate myself at a party in front of my friends.

I had pain pent up for years and years. Now, I look back at my problems and laugh about them, but as an irrational, immature teenager, I thought my problems were the end of the world!

Problems like the girls I liked not wanting to date me. My friends were not cool enough. I did not wear the best clothes. I did not have the coolest car. My only hobby was smoking weed. My dad and I were not getting along because of his wife and new kids. My mother and I were not getting along because we never did. I was doing pretty bad in school. There was so much wrapped up into me, and I had no one I could talk to. I never trusted my friends, teachers, or family enough to talk to them.

Things as simple as these are all it takes to drive a teenager over the edge. I knew many kids who tried to kill themselves before I did. Many of them looked like they had it all. I heard many stories of star high school football players and high school basketball protégés committing suicide. I thought those kids would be the last people to ever consider killing themselves, but they were not. It turns out that many teens are upset and saddened with themselves and their environments. Considering it is hard to change your environment, and just about as hard to change yourself, it seems almost logical that a teenager would consider suicide a viable means of escaping their condition.

Many teenagers feel hopeless when they realize that soon enough they really have to move out of their homes and start life on their own. That pressure is enough to bust the bubble of parental security they are used to hiding in for so long. All of a sudden the world that once revolved around your son meets reality when he turns 17 and he only has about 14 or 15 months to get his life in order. I dare to say that at least 50 percent of all teenagers, of all races, of all genders, and of all backgrounds have contemplated taking their own lives at least once, but many of them would never admit it.

What is the problem? I believe the problem among all teenagers concerning suicide is a lack of being in touch with oneself. Many teenagers are trying to get in touch with everyone else, such as their friends, boyfriends, girlfriends, et cetera.

They are so busy trying to get to know and connect with everyone else that they fail to get to know and connect with themselves. They cling to someone else for support, and then once that person abandons or separates from them the teens lose it.

Many who were never *whole* attempt to make themselves whole by adding themselves to someone else. That type of behavior only keeps a person *whole* while that bond is together. Once the other person is taken away, it leaves the teenager alone. Many teens feel unloved or abandoned when their friends leave them or their parents hurt them. They lose it and go to the extreme. Usually the incidents leading up to the suicidal incident happen more then once, causing the teen to believe that he or she is unfit for love or life.

There are many causes of suicide for teenagers:
- Feeling misplaced within society. For example, African-American kids in predominately White neighborhoods can begin to feel like they do not belong, and may take on an inferiority complex.
- Family issues
- School pressures
- Gang related
- Drug related
- Relationship related
- Depression
- Social loneliness
- Difficulty coping with neighborhood. Some males in rougher neighborhoods, superficial neighborhoods, or in overly sophisticated environments may have their pride broken. A man without pride is not alive.

The list is as long as there are different personalities and different circumstances. Below is a list of things you as a mother should be aware of should you suspect suicide could be a problem. Please do not get worried and begin thinking everything your son does on this list is a sign of suicide. The fact is that many teenagers, when going through their inner struggles, will show many of these signs. The difference is the severity and the longevity of the signs.
- Constantly sleeping no matter what time of day or how long he has slept before.
- Trouble eating for an extended period of time, and rapid weight loss (or weight gain).
- Drastic behavior changes.
- Extreme substance abuse. Increased use of alcohol or drugs. This goes into the subject of "slow suicide." Slow suicide is when a person lives a base

lifestyle knowing that their way of life is going to eventually put them six feet in the dirt. They continue to live that lifestyle regardless. Many kids do this with alcohol, cigarettes, sex, drugs, and the like.
- Total withdrawal from friends and social activities.
- Giving away prized possessions, ex: baseball cards, CDs, favorite clothes.
- Extensive poetry or journal writing. Not a poet or songwriter, but the boy who has his head stuffed in headphones all of the time writing things he will not let anybody read.
- Loss of interest in everything, ex: hobbies, school, dating, TV.
- Loss of interest in maintaining his personal appearance.
- Mentioning suicide in a conversation, whether deliberately or unintentionally.

Many parents feel that their kid will never consider suicide. It is discomforting to think about. Maybe you just cannot bring yourself to believe it, but it is dangerous for your son if you continue to ignore the idea that he might be suicidal. I am shy of recommending being so forward as to ask your son openly if he wants to or has thought about killing himself. If he has or is and you burst his bubble you may spin him into a rage, and if he has not or is not then you may offend him and drive a wedge between you two. Instead, I recommend you stay vigilant and listen to his non-verbal indicators.

For example, what kind of music is he listening to? In my case, I had a phase in my life when I listened to crazy death-talking rock and roll music as a teenaged black male. That was not the only music I listened to, but for this example it is important. I did drugs, avoided many social activities, separated myself from people, and stayed very quiet for a long time. Those signs are enough to at least bring up the radar that something is wrong. Remember, music is saying the words that he wishes he could say, but may not be brave enough to say yet. Music reflects personality. Crazy, loose-screw music usually equals crazy, loose-screw personalities. "F the world" music speaks for itself.

Maybe what he is watching on TV can give you a clue to what is going on with him. If you find he is fascinated with death that may raise a red flag or two.

A large number of black people feel it is taboo to speak about suicide. We have this stigma on the word, and believe it is only for white people, but the stats do not support that belief. African Americans have to begin opening their eyes and get involved with these teenagers' lives. Do not lecture and lecture, but be genuinely interested. Be open to listen. Always make sure that your son knows how much you love him and how important he is. Do the same for his friends too. Help another mother out.

SUICIDE

In addition, I have noticed that a proper level of responsibility drives away feelings of suicide. The more a person feels needed the less likely they are to want to kill themselves. If your son has a job in the home, some major responsibility like providing for the home or for little brothers or sisters, then he will be less likely to take his life. *The responsibilities in his life will drive him to keep living, but when he has nothing to live for and nothing to drive for, he has no reason to live.* A word of caution on this however. The responsibility needs to come before the suicidal tendencies appear not afterward. If you load an already depressed youth with more strain and pressure you will only increase his anxiety and discomfort.

When suicidal tendencies are present, I recommend seeking help. I recommend reading books and becoming aware on the subject of suicide. I asked a few of my friends if they had ever considered suicide. Personally, I was shocked to hear I was not the only one who considered suicide to escape this life. There is definitely a problem. Not only is your son at risk, but his friends, your friends' kids, and your relatives' kids are at risk. You have to get involved or the stats will continue to rise–for every race.

This suicide issue among teenagers has a lot to do with a lack of strong role models, but adults have hundreds of role models and they commit suicide, so that cannot be the only issue and problem. The problem is deeper. The problem is often the deep-rooted feelings of hopelessness and loneliness that come from a lack of self-esteem. The objective, parents, quite simply is to destroy every chance for your son to feel hopeless or lonely or severely depressed and abandoned. Destroy feelings of inadequacy, loneliness, helplessness, and fear of the future. There are many ways to do this, but the best are: Giving your son responsibility, taking him traveling, and building him a plan for his future that makes his life worth living in the present.

Mothers, if you suspect a problem, contact any suicide help agency before it is too late. Talk to your son's teachers and find out how he is getting along with kids at school. Find out what his public personality is like and what type of friends he hangs around with at school. Do everything that you can to keep your son alive.

Remember not to excite frenzy inside of yourself and begin interrogating your child to find out if he is suicidal. Chances are that he has thought about it, but he has never gone all the way through with the act. Just love him. Let him know you love him, and work on providing the best opportunities that you can for him.

Above all else, know that it is not your fault if he should decide to take his own life. No matter what you do, you cannot control all his actions. He is a free spirit, free to live or die as he sees fit. Yes, it will undoubtedly hurt you, but do not ever feel embarrassed or ashamed as a mother. I know it sounds cold hearted of me to say, but I say it for your own protection–the protection of your own heart. If you

allow your son's suicidal act to take control of your emotions, the pain, the embarrassment, the hurt could actually drive you to follow suit. I pray no mother ever has to be in this situation.
Remember to listen to non-verbal clues. Get involved in his life right now and never stop. Do not badger him about how important life is. Instead, give him important responsibilities. Do your best to eradicate any of the causes of suicide. Lastly, remember that if you suspect suicide, get help before it is too late. Always seek professional help if you suspect suicide to be a reality in your son's life. Do not guess or think that he will not do it, because he just might. Do not worry about the money, worry about your son's life! When talking to a counselor, ask if you can bring in one of your child's friends to talk to the counselor. The friend is likely to add insight about your son's actions outside of the home. This would greatly benefit the counselor since neither you nor the doctor know what is going on, since your son most likely will not talk. A friend of your son's will be willing to help save his friend's life. You just have to be willing to reach out to that kid for help.

Chapter Twenty-one

The Boy's Father

Sometimes we fall into situations and circumstances we would rather not be in, but complaining about them is not going to help at all.

- Cederick W. Tardy II

Many people have no idea just how much power they have in their words. They forget on occasion. Many times we all forget that the things we say are the things we believe, and that our beliefs form our environments. Often times, many single mothers forget just how much power they have in their words too. They forget because their kids do not always listen to them, or their ex-husband or boss may treat them less than or ignore them.

In this absentmindedness, many single mothers slip up and say some awfully hurtful things to their children. Unaware of the negative repercussions placed upon their son's lives when they make these harsh comments, often times a single mother will say something totally uncalled for about their child's biological father. I say unaware because, if they were truly aware and understood the magnitude of the impact their words had on their son, they would never ever talk badly about the child's father in the child's presence.

This chapter is going to focus on the power of the mother's words, the vulnerability of the child's thinking, and the actions the mother could consider when speaking about the father.

Many people do not understand how powerful their voice and speech are, so do not think I am saying only women do not know. Many people fail to realize that our memories hold on to the smallest details for our entire lives. We especially remember all of the negative things that happened in our lifetime. A good point for single mothers to remember is that every word that you speak in your home and to your child matters a great deal. The words you speak to anyone matter, but especially to your child.

The words we speak matter because they are remembered, maybe not by us, but by someone. Someone always remembers what we have to say. They remember the words we spoke years ago as if they just happened. For example, Dr. Martin Luther King's "I Have a Dream" speech is still remembered years after he delivered it. What you say to your son may not be as groundbreaking as what Dr. King had to say, but the same principle applies. People, especially your own children, will remember what you say for years, and possibly forever. Think about it. How many random things can you remember that a friend said in high school, an employee said at work, or that someone said in the line at the grocery store? We remember a lot.

Your son, even though he has not yet developed the adult brain that you have, still remembers *a lot*. Remember earlier when I said that the words you speak matter, especially to your own child? Let me explain why. When you conceived your son, there was something stronger then an umbilical cord tying the two of you together. The bond that can only be built between mother and son was there, and despite the fights, arguments, and foul words, that bond has never left. That bond will never leave. Even after one of you has passed on, the other will feel that bond. The bond between a mother and son is strong, stronger then any steel. Steel can be broken, but the love of a mother for her son and vice versa is eternal.

It is because of this bond that the words you speak to your son hold more weight than you may think. Ever since your son was born, his first instincts told him that you were there for him, and that he could trust you. He cried for you as a baby and you came running. He cried for you as a toddler and you were there. You were always there to protect and serve him, and he has trusted you ever since.

Things in the household may be different now. You may not feel any bond and you may not feel any trust, but that basic instinct is still there. Because of this bond and instinctive trust, when you speak to him, whether positively or negatively, your words do not have to overcome the same barriers as when his teachers speak to him or his friends speak to him. They do not have the same instinctive bond that you two do. Your words skip all the conscious thoughts and guards and go right into his heart. Whether your words are good or bad, they go directly into his heart, because he has instinctively trusted you since he was born.

You are his mother. When you speak, the mother and son bond makes what you say the "truth" to him, good or bad. When you say, "I know you can do it," it skips the thought process and goes straight into his heart. But, you often have to rebuke your child more than inspire him. Instead of "You can do it," the child might hear something like, "You are acting just as sorry as your father!" You may fly off the cuff one day and say, "That is why I do not like you, you look just like your daddy." I have heard mothers tell their kids that they were never going to be anything just like their daddy is never going to be anything.

I thank God my mother never said things like this to me, but that does not mean I can skip around the topic. If you have ever said anything that has any resemblance to those types of statements, you need to keep reading, and hopefully you will be convinced to change your ways for your son's sakes. And, if you have never said anything like this to your child and never will, you should still continue reading, because one day you will run across a single mother who needs this advice.

Let's recap to make sure we do not lose anyone. The words you speak to your son have a greater impact on him because of the instinctive bond built early in childhood. When you say that your son is just like his father, that he is never going to be anything just like his father, that he looks retarded just like his father, or something to that nature, it is going to be first remembered, and then it is going to find its way into your son's heart and actions.

He will remember your harsh words voiced to him about his father. It is human nature to remember the negatives in life before remembering the positives. It is also human nature to replay those negative memories over and over and over again in the imagination. All those pathetic things you told him will constantly echo in his brain forever, or until he gets the strength to get over them.

It is a proven fact that what we allow to enter our minds influences our actions. It is a proven fact that what we hear the most will weigh the heaviest on our minds, and our minds have the say so on our actions.

The things we hear most influence how we think. This is why you as mothers have to be especially careful about what you say. If you are constantly telling your children negative things like, "You are sorry just like your father," those thoughts will soon get into your son's heart, and from his heart, they will become his actions. Even if you are thinking, "Well, I have only said something like that once or twice. I do not do it all the time," it does not matter. It does not matter if you said it once or a hundred times, because the child's memory has already captured what was said, and like a bad sitcom, it replays what you said over and over and over again for years and years. When he tries to sleep, he is bombarded with those harsh thoughts, night after night, and when he fails a quiz at school that is the first thought in his mind. You do not have to continue to tell him, because when you do it once, his mind will repeat it for you.

"You sorry little bastard! I knew he should have worn a condom. You were a mistake." If you say something like that to your child, you have just messed his head up for years to come. Every time he makes a mistake from then on those words will replay on cue.

The mother-son bond causes him to take something so harsh and negative and make it a part of his memory. The things you say, especially the negative things you say, go into his ears, past the defense barriers, straight to his heart and mind, then travel from his mind to his thoughts and beliefs. His thoughts and beliefs produce his actions. *You can use this positively or negatively.* You can decide to pump his little brain full of positive messages or you can pump his brain full of junk. The principle is going to work either way, so you must be careful about what you say, especially about the child's father. If you need to cuss about the father or release some aggression about the father, that is normal, but do it away from your child–no matter how old he is.

Let me explain to you why it is so imperative that you refrain from bad-mouthing the boy's father in front of him. First let me put it in a math problem: Mom + Dad = Boy

You, plus the dad, equal your son. That makes that man half of your son. When you tear down the father, it is symbolic to tearing down half of your son. That is why it is so important to refrain from verbally demolishing the father in the child's presence. It would be like you having a delicious chocolate sundae and then someone you love coming by and spitting on it. It would ruin your day! Amplify that feeling as high as you feel you need to in order to make ruined ice cream compare to a ruined image of a father, then you will be able to perceive the amount of pain and depression caused by these negative actions.

I have heard some single mothers tell me that they bond with their son by bashing his father. I always walk away from conversations like this, but in my head I think, "There is no way this could be a good situation." It just doesn't make sense to a rational mind. Even if you can bond with your son in that manner, why would you? That is like bonding with your son over a line of cocaine. Great that you two found something you enjoy, but in the end, it is more destructive than good. Bond with your son with positive relationship-building devices, and watch your son develop into a man. Bond with your son in a negative manner, and watch your son turn and do the same thing his father did to another woman when he is older.

Talking badly about the father does little good, and can only make you look ignorant. Your son, especially if he is of the age where he can put two and two together, will be thinking, "If my father is such a bad person, why did you have sex with him?" Your son will soon start to lose respect for you and your entire decision-making process.

The child's father is not a scapegoat. When things are going wrong financially, you cannot cop out and use the father as a scapegoat. You cannot blame all the problems on the father, especially if he is not even around, because you then would be ignoring the fact you played a role in the situation. If the father is not paying his child support, relax, get the court involved, get your money legally, and go on about your business. Cut your living expenses down to meet your income, do what you have to do, because blaming the father will get nothing done at all. Use your energy to bust your butt, get a raise and a promotion, and start taking care of your business.

Do not force your child into thinking his father is a deadbeat by throwing out little tidbits about how sorry his dad is. Let the child figure it out on his own. When I was really young, my dad used to tell me that he would come pick me up on the weekends and then never show. My mother could have used that as ammunition to shoot my father into the dirt, but she rarely did that. Soon, I came to the realization on my own about my father's actions.

You do not have to be the sponsor of negative feelings about a deadbeat father. Your son will figure it out on his own. You just be there to support him. When he is old enough, his eyes will open and see the real truth. He will see who was there all the time and who was not, and he will respect you for it. Now, do not expect that to happen anytime soon, but it will happen.

My purpose in writing these books is to help you become the best mother, and not a like-all-the-rest mother. I have told you a lot about what you should not do, so now I want to give insight into the things you can and should consider doing. The tips below will not only help your son through the situation, but they will help you deal with it better as well. As you delve into the entire situation and see it clearly, a lot of the stress will roll right off of your back.

Here are some things that you can do regarding the father: You can educate your son about his father. You can do this whenever he asks about him, whenever you are comfortable, or when you put this book down. All you will do is explain to him about his other half. I recommend putting it all out on the table. Well, maybe not all, but everything he needs to know. Let him ask you questions, and be open to answering them.

Before you do this, make a list of everything that you would like to say to your son about his father. Making a list does two things. One, it makes sure you get it all out on the table so later on you don't remember something you wish you had said. Two, it allows you to stay on topic. If you feel yourself drifting too far off the point and rambling on, you can get yourself restructured by looking at the list.

If you have pictures of his father, they would be excellent, especially if he has never seen him. If the father died, try to find newspaper clippings or something to shed light on the experience. All of this will only take about an hour or two of work for you, but the end will be priceless. Explain everything that you have, and explain everything that you do not have. Be honest and real with him. Do not be so real that your son can no longer respect you because you told him more then he should know, but be real with him about his father.

If the father is around, worth talking to, and is *willing* to spend one-on-one time with his son, allow your son to talk with him personally about what happened

THE BOY'S FATHER

in the past. That does not allow you to skip your talk with your son, but instead affords your son the opportunity to get both sides of the story. When you do this though, make sure you do not tell your son anything about his father you would not want repeated to his father, because many times kids can say more than they should. If the terms of the separation are so harsh that they do not allow your son to speak with his father, do your best to explain why that is.

If your son starts asking you a lot of questions it is because he is interested. If he is not, he may still be interested, just uncomfortable. Do not worry either way. Just keep doing what you know is right, despite how he feels, like when my mother used to make me go to church even when I was high. She knew it was right and she kept doing what she knew was right despite how I felt about it, and it paid off.

Some single mothers hate their ex-man so badly that they do not even talk about him. Never leave it up to your son to wonder about who his father is. He is going to want to know something about the other half of him. Either he will find out on his own, or his imagination will make something up, which could be devastating. Let your son spend his time, energy, and imagination thinking about success, learning, and searching for opportunity, not looking for his dad.

Just remember to watch what you say, because what you say weighs *heavily* on your son's heart and mind, which weighs *heavily* on his thoughts and beliefs, which weighs *heavily* on his actions, which weighs *heavily* on and dictate his future.

Chapter Twenty-two

The Difference Between Working Hard in the Family and Working Hard for the Family

Priorities for one may not be priorities for another, but for any mother, her number one priority needs to be her child.

- Cederick W. Tardy II

This is a true story. When I was a child, around 12 years old, I had a lot of friends who lived in my neighborhood. There was one kid in particular, a little younger than I was, who lived down the street. We used to hang out with each other every day, but one day I noticed that I had never met his parents. I came to find out that his parents recently divorced and he lived with his mother. What a coincidence. We both were being raised by single mothers.

When we were at this age we were not even thinking about drugs, skipping school, or partying. This boy from down the street and I hung out together the most because everyone else's parents would make them do their homework before they could go outside. *Since we didn't have parents at home telling us to do our homework we just hung out all day long together.*

Both of our mothers worked long nights so we would play video games until pretty late at night. We did pretty much whatever we wanted to do. There was no one else there to stop us. One day we fabricated a scheme to break our parents' liquor bottles after we had consumed the contents, and then tell our parents we accidently broke the bottles and cleaned up the alcohol. We were able to do this type of stuff because no one was there to watch us.

Both of our parents worked late, as I said, but I took notice that his mother would not come home until really late at night. Sometimes his mom would not come home until two or three in the morning. I found out that his mother had gotten breast implants since the last time anyone else had seen her, and became a stripper for a local club. I guess since she was single, young, and fairly attractive, she figured she would do what she could to make extra money for the household.

This shocked everyone in the neighborhood because none of us had ever met a stripper before. We were just kids. The only thing close to that in my book was meeting a guy when I was around 8 or 9 whose wife was a Dallas Cowboys cheerleader. But a stripper? This was the news of the neighborhood! After all the neighborhood kids found out, they told their parents. Then their parents told everyone else's parents. Soon the kid became an outcast. Everyone made fun of him. We would talk about having sex with his mother or leaving money behind for her. You know how mean kids can be? We were pretty harsh on him, but the neighborhood parents were just as harsh. Many of the parents ordered their kids to stay away from his house because they believed his mother was some kind of sexual predator.

I guess that all of this pressure and the fact his mom was never home really got to this boy. He ended up going from a normal pre-teenage kid to a bit of a problem child. He went from good to bad due to everything that was happening in his life. His mother was never home to console him. He started to get in a lot of trouble at school and around the neighborhood. Not too long after this they packed up and moved. Where they went I do not know to this day, because I have never seen or heard from him again. I pray everything turned out the better for him, and I apologize for the things I said to him about his mother, but that can only do so much. Around the time all of this was happening with his mother, my mother was also working late nights. She was working side jobs to make ends meet. I was scared she was a stripper for a moment! The rumors began, but they soon fizzled out. My mother was working a network-marketing program as a side job along with a full time job.

With a full-time job and network marketing on the side, my mother would sometimes not come home on weekdays until well after 11 at night. Many nights I would stay up and protect the house with my BB gun. The weekends were the only times I ever got to see her. She would always make time to take me to get my haircut. As we would ride across town to my favorite barber, she would always ask me what was wrong. It seemed I would sit in the passenger seat and mope constantly. Really I did not know what was wrong. I had no idea that all these circumstances and events were leading up to the violent downward spiral my life would succumb to over the next few years.

I would tell her my problem was that I never got to see her anymore. She would always reply that her long hours were only going to be a temporary nuisance. She would say things like, "I am doing this for you. If I did not do this we would not have this nice car, nice house, these nice clothes, and everything else." In my head I would think about the material things and weigh them against the relationship I was having with my mother. Funny, even at such a young age I knew that what she was saying just did not sound right.

Though I knew the truth, I would smile and think about the future when all my mother's long hours would pay off. We both dreamed of a day when she would not have to work so much, and possibly even work from home. We would both smile in the car, dreaming about how great the future was going to be. But as the years passed, the hope faded with them.

Year after year my mother was still working long hours, and the financial problems seemed to only get worse. It seemed like the more she worked, the less money we had. To make it even worse, I was becoming a teenager now. I was unsupervised nearly every day for years and moving on to high school.

In high school, I started doing drugs and skipping school. I was acting like a complete fool. I never learned the importance of doing my homework right after school. Once riding bikes grew old, the next biggest thing was doing drugs and selling drugs after school. By the time my mother realized she had spent those key developmental years of my life working at achieving financial stability instead of spending an adequate amount of time teaching, training, and raising her son, it was too late for me. It was way too late. As I said earlier, we both had no idea whatsoever that those years prior to my downward spiral were going to cause me to do so miserably and turn so far left.

I am sure that we both thought I would be fine taking care of myself as my mom worked to pay the bills. We both thought that she would work and make the money and I would be fine. Little did we know that by the time I was 15 years old things would start sinking fast. Once she realized what had happened it was too late to do anything but start the damage control process. Damage control is a term that means controlling chaos. How many of us know that it is difficult at best to control chaos?

As a mother, your parenting strategy should never become one of damage control. Yes, you will have to fix problems from time to time, and it is always crucial to know how to fix what has gone wrong in your life, but damage control is a last option, not the only. You should be using a damage prevention or damage avoidance strategy to better the life of you and your son. Believe me, when it comes down to the point of fixing what is wrong, it could very well be too late.

There are a lot of things I could touch on in the true story you just read, and I hope you were able to pick up on the issues that I have not addressed in this book. What I want to point out from the story about two young boys with single mothers who worked late nights leaving their boys unattended is that both of them turned from good kids to bad kids in a very short time.

Both of us, the boy from down the street and I, were not terribly bad kids when we met each other, but after being left unsupervised for so long, we found ourselves lost on the wrong side of the track. Moreover, in both cases, by the time our mothers addressed the situation it was too late. This chapter will hopefully give single mothers some insight into the effects of working hard to provide for their family, but neglecting working hard in the family

Many single mothers who are the sole providers for their home have to work hard at their jobs, because if they lose their job their son will suffer. But, many mothers forget that they must be working just as hard in their families, keeping them intact, if they wish to have a family to provide for in the future. There is a big difference between working hard to provide for the family and working hard in the family. Both are important, but when there is an imbalance on either side, the effects are drastic. On one hand, working too hard at work will leave your child unattended and left up to his own devices. On the other hand, working too little may get you fired and leave you in a poverty-stricken situation.

How I wish that my mother had known the difference between working hard to provide for me and working hard to build a relationship with me. How I wish that she had realized which was truly the most important 10 or 15 years ago. If I had told her the truth all those years ago in the car on the way to the barber shop, would I have had to write this book? If only we would have known how terrible this chain of events would become or what I would become.

What if she had known that I would have been just as happy in a small apartment with the basics and my mother around more often, than I was with a new house and no mother. Please do not confuse my statements with being ungrateful or cold hearted. Neither would be true. The truth is I thank my mother every day for everything she did. She did what she thought was best, and in the end it all worked out, so I never want anyone to assume that I am ungrateful. The purpose of addressing this issue is to warn everyone reading this that many kids who grew up like the boy down the street and I can give similar testimonies of downward spirals caused by a lack of supervision and a lack of relationship with their mothers, but not all of them can give a testimony of a life change.

If my mother had known that the years of work she exerted to provide the material things in our lives were tearing a scar deeper then we both knew could exist, would she have done the same thing over again? Her working hard turned out to be counterproductive to her goal of raising a healthy son with all his needs met. As I stated, many more boys can give you the same story. Their parents, like mine, figured that they needed to work hard to maintain a good-paying job, and figured the child was "old enough to take care of himself." This issue is more of a suburban, middle-class, hyper-consumer family issue than anything else. I believe this because many middle-class families work harder at medium income jobs so that they can buy the things the have always wanted. Many times they buy more things than they can afford and end up having to work even harder to pay them off. Whether this issue is the cause or not studies will show, but the result of the behavior is evident.

All of us young men who are still around to tell our stories would explain those years of life like rolling down a path with no brakes and no way to steer ourselves. We all were moving too fast in life with no guidance.

Imagine it like this: A car is sitting on top of a hill in neutral and begins to roll down the hill. If there is no one inside to steer it around the turns it needs to make it will not make it past the first turn. Instead, it will gain speed rapidly as it barrels down the hill, the car will miss the turn, veer sharply in the wrong direction, and eventually damage itself in a collision. *Not only will the car get damaged, but everything it comes into contact with will be damaged as well, all because it was neglected.* Someone set that car on that hill, thinking, "It will not go anywhere. It will be fine by itself."

Mothers, my life and the lives of many other single mother's sons are analogous to that car. Left to run on our own, we found ourselves running full speed with no guidance. Once we missed that first turn in life, we found ourselves barreling off into the unknown about to face some nasty collisions with the forces of life. Not only did I damage myself back then, but I damaged everyone I came into contact with. Those who would tell their stories would say that they damaged girls by getting them pregnant or hurt some innocent person that they robbed.

Thankfully, God was able to show me how to grab hold of the wheel and steer myself into safety, but not everyone has been or will be so fortunate. Many of the young men sitting in prison right now were the ones who were not so fortunate. Many of the young boys with children are examples of how a kid left to his own devices will never make the right decision.

So what do you do, mothers? How can you prevent the damage rather than fix the damage once it has occurred? I am sure you have an inclination of what you could do. My best advice to you is to write your inclination down next to this paragraph, and then begin to make that thought a reality. Do not just let that thought disappear, because that thought just might be the thought that saves your boy's life! I got jumped, car jacked, and left stranded in a train yard with my best friend, left there to die as a train approached, all because we were left unattended for so long.

Mothers, whatever you know you need to do to prevent this from happening to your son I beg of you to do it and do it now, but do not just assume everything will be all right. That is a lie. If you happen to be working more then one job or working so many hours that you hardly see your son, that may be the biggest reason you are having trouble raising him or it may become the issue. Your absence will cause you to become like another adult stranger in his young eyes. My advice is that you seek an alternate means of making a living so that you can be there for your son in those crucial developmental years. If you cannot possibly find an alternative means of making a living then I suggest that you cut back on your expenses so that you do not have to work such long hours to pay for things.

Remember that working hard to provide for your family is important, but working hard in the family is crucial. Your hard work may end up becoming counterproductive to your goal of providing for your son.

Let us say that as a single mother you live this hypothetical day below:
- Work from 9 a.m. -5 p.m.
- Fight traffic all the way home
- Get home around 7 p.m. or 7:30 p.m.
- Extremely tired, you may cook or watch TV
- Go to sleep by 10 o'clock
- Wake up at 6:30 a.m. to be at work by 9 a.m.
- Repeat this cycle day after day

Every human has the same 24 hours in a day. The average human sleeps for eight of those hours, and works for eight of those hours. The average human showers and dresses for one of those hours, transits to and from work for two of those hours, and eats for one and half of those hours. Right there, that is 20 and a half hours of your day gone to normal human duties. Then the average person talks on the phone, watches TV, reads, exercises, or does any number of things to fill in the remaining three and a half hours in their day. The point I am trying to make is you have *three and a half hours*.

Let us examine this because it is important. If all you have is three and a half hours a day that are not already accounted for, what could or should you be doing with them as a single mother? Exercise and reading are definitely important, but I beg you to consider using those three and half hours spending quality time with your son instead of on the non-essential matters of life. Begin investing the little time you do have into your son's development, because that investment will pay off better then any stock or bond.

If that made clear sense to you, you are ready to raise a wonderful young man who will be an asset to society.

Let me also point out that many of you do not have to work on weekends, and it is not required that you spend that entire three and a half hours a day with your child. Realistically, you will have to wind down after your workday, and even take an hour or two to yourself so that you do not lose your sanity. This is all right, but remember that your son will "lose control of the wheel" if he is left steering himself through life. You do not have to spend your only three free hours with your son every day. You can fill two of his unaccounted for hours with a sport, hobby, or something constructive that will keep his mind focused while you handle your business.

Whatever you decide to do, never fall into the trap of believing he will be able to raise himself. *Your son spends those same eight hours that you spend at work, at school, surrounded by negative influences. If he is left up to his own judgment, he will spend the rest of his 16 hours drowning in those same influences.*

On the weekdays, if you were to spend an hour a day with him, you could plan to work on homework one day, the latest issue of life the next, working out the next, or even planning a weekend activity. On the weekends you should free your schedule every other weekend so that you two can spend it together doing what the two of you like to do best. On the other weekends, you can let him stay with a friend and you can spend that time with a boyfriend or working on your goals.

As I said many times, if I had only told my mom the truth on the way to the barber shop that a relationship with her was more important than the passing material things life had to offer, who knows where I would be. Had we only known that the events I spoke about would have led to the terrible downward spiral I found myself falling into, I know we would have done all we could to prevent it from happening.

Remember the story of the boy whose mother was a stripper and how he turned out, and remember that there are many boys just like us who can give you the same story. I thank God that He was able to catch me before I went too far down that wrong path, but not every boy is so fortunate. You must work hard to provide for your family, but never let providing provisions become the avenue for neglect. Your son's life needs you behind the wheel. He needs your guidance. You have three and a half hours in your day to invest in your son. Do it right and it will pay off better then any blue chip stock.

Chapter Twenty-three

The Greatest Compliments Come From Your Son

Nothing resolves a tumultuous situation like compromise.
- Cederick W. Tardy II

In our society, many of us have become so accustomed to achieving a level where we receive praise from a boss that we almost consider it a goal. We think, "I am going to do this with all I have that way the boss will be sure to notice me!" We function and therefore assume that our lives revolve around pleasing these figures. We live a life constantly in pursuit of that next "good job," handshake, or pat on the back. This is not to knock anyone for his or her behaviors, just go with me. Think about how we strive at work to have someone tell us "Good job!"

Sometimes we even go as far as to give ourselves appreciation when others fail to recognize our valiant efforts. In this pursuit of appreciation and compliments from an authority figure, I believe that many mothers can forget that the greatest compliment she will ever hear will only come from her own child.

Imagine this next literary picture as your life.

You wake up at 7 o'clock in the morning to go to work. You do not have to be in until 9, so you take the time to beautify yourself. You dress yourself nicely, and your makeup accents your face exquisitely. You leave your home at about 8 o'clock feeling good about your appearance. You check yourself over a few more times before getting to your office.

Once you make it to the parking lot, you step out of your car, grab your bag, press the alarm, and put on your "Good Morning Face." You greet the same people as you did the day before, but this morning someone was courteous enough to compliment you on how beautiful you look this morning. You thank them and return the compliment. As you walk away from that occurrence, you notice that you feel even better about yourself at that moment. However, that feeling soon fades, because you realize that most compliments from a coworker are merely common courtesy and are rarely sincere.

The day has only just begun and your manager is already piling loads of work on the corner of your desk. He explains that one of your coworkers is out sick for

The Greatest Compliments

the day, and he needs you to take up that person's slack. You smile, shuffle the papers, and reluctantly accept. As the day goes by, you notice that you have been extremely efficient, completing your work and your coworker's load as well. As your boss leaves for the day, he decides to check up on you. "Wow," he says, "you got everything done! You are the greatest! What would I do without you?" He tells you all the nice jobs he could possibly formulate, shakes your hand, pats you on the back, and even makes a promise to make this burden up to you.

As you walk away from that occurrence, you notice that you feel better about yourself at that moment. However, that feeling soon fades, because you realize that most compliments from a manager are merely common courtesy and are rarely sincere.

You leave the office, get back into your car, close the door and sigh, thankful that another day is over. On the drive home, you happen to let a driver merge into your lane despite how terrible the traffic is. You look straight ahead, and notice a "thank you wave" from the driver you just let merge. You smile and wave back, feeling good, as if you have done a good deed. However, that good feeling soon fades, because you realize that most compliments that come from a total stranger are merely common courtesy and are rarely ever sincere.

Later on that drive home, you realize that it is Thursday, your day to cook a meal for your boyfriend at your home. You two decided early in the relationship that you would cook for one another once a week and serve each other like distinguished guests. Excited, you rush into the house and begin your valiant clean up effort. You cook a wonderful meal of grilled red snapper with lemon butter sauce, sautéed vegetables, and rice pilaf with a tossed garden salad and rolls. You serve your boyfriend, clean up after him, and you make sure that next week he has to top you. You did a good job. His praises, thank yous, compliments, and pleasant words only boost your high. Elated you sit back and enjoy a nice foot massage. As wonderful as this makes you feel, this feeling soon fades too, because in your heart you know something is missing.

Almost like clockwork your son pokes his pointy head out of his room. "Mom, I need help with my homework!" he yells. You sigh. You do not want to leave your foot massage, but your boyfriend winks at you, letting you know that you have a more important responsibility to take care of. With ease, you solve your son's homework problem, making you look like Super Woman! With joy, he hugs you, and says, "Thank you" only once before he runs back into his room.

As you walk back into the living room to rejoin your boyfriend and return to your massage, you notice that that good feeling has not yet faded. In fact, that good feeling has made you feel like everything you did throughout your day was worth it. You feel like a bona fide mother, whole, as if that one thank you was all you were missing in your day. See? That compliment that your son gives you, though he only has to say it once, is authentic. That good feeling you get from it remains for a long, long time.

This fictional day may sound far-fetched to many of you. It is a little far-fetched for even myself, but is that to say that many of the things that happened that day have not or could not happen in your life? Of course not, because many times we go through events such as the ones above.

Let us examine two issues. For starters, I would like to point out that the compliment that came from the mother's son made her feel special, whole, and genuine as a mother. Second, most mothers will never receive a compliment from their sons at all. We can assume that the boy in the fictional story is young, but what about if your son is older, in junior high or high school?

It is my belief that no other compliment can make you feel the way that a compliment from your son can make you feel. Deep down you know that when an adult gives you praise, many times it is out of mere kindness and not sincerity, but when a child or anyone under the age of 19 compliments you it is a big deal. Compliments, especially in my generation, seem to have gone the way of the cassette tape. They are hard to find and even harder to find someone who still uses them.

When you can get a child or anyone under 19 to say, "You did a great job!" or "Thank you!" without being told to, then you know that you have truly done something precious. A compliment from an adolescent is rare. Therefore, the compliments you receive from your son should make you feel like all your hard work for your child's life has been worthwhile.

Imagine the day your son thanks you sincerely for your hard work. We often go through life chasing empty desires and wishing upon stars. We chase the wind hoping one day to find where it came from. We cry out for answers only to find we knew them all along. We look for fulfillment in so many areas in life. Many times we even look in the same area more then once for what cannot be found there. We search for completeness in relationships with the opposite sex, but all too often, those wonderful emotions quickly turn into bitterness. We try finding fulfillment in food, only to wind up hungry once more. We try to find fulfillment in alcohol, only to sober up once again. We try to find fulfillment in sex, only to get horny again. We try friends, but soon they grow annoying, and the people at church can be awfully irritating. We try to find fulfillment in all of these things, and often we try more than once.

You, as a mother, are luckier than you realize. You have a special place to look for fulfillment. *When you work for your company it raises the company's bottom line, but when you work at home, raising your son, it raises a man.* That is fulfilling.

This is why I believe you must be working just as hard to receive compliments from your son as you do to receive compliments from your boss, manager, boyfriend, pastor, fiancé, or others. Yes, it is wonderful when you receive praise and admiration from these people, and we should never become negative about receiving compliments from these people. Instead, we must never forget to work equally hard to get our son's compliments.

So what is the hold-up? Why haven't you put this book down and gone to work in your son's life in order to get the compliments?

My suspicion is that you believe no matter what you do, your son will never compliment you. You figure he is too mature, too hard, too masculine, or just too hardheaded to compliment you. I believe there are three main reasons why many mothers never hear a compliment from their sons. First, their actions as a mother may not be worth complimenting at this stage. Two, their boy may not understand the value of a compliment because he was never taught. Three, their son may just be too hardheaded!

It is my belief that most mothers who never get a sincere, flattering comment of praise from their sons believe that type of behavior is normal for a teenage boy, and therefore they never correct his behavior. Whether this is always the case or not, one truth is that many mothers get no appreciation because they have not shown themselves worthy of being praised.

If that upset you please take a breath and calm down. Relax–before you get so upset that you read right past the answers you have been looking for.

Remember that a child is selfish, and being a selfish individual, he will not interpret your efforts at your place of employment as meaningful to him. Your job is one thing, but he wants to see what you do at home, specifically for him. If you are not doing the things that he requires from you then you honestly have no valid grounds for expecting appreciation. This is when parents turn to demanding appreciation, which is always a negative. The way to find out what you need to do in order to receive gratitude and thanks from your son is simply ask him what he thinks you should be doing. Simply ask him, because he is the only one who knows what he wants.

By no means do you have to do everything he requests of you, unless the requests are levelheaded and would actually make you a better mother. I do not suggest that you should buy your son a race car and the newest pairs of shoes if he asks, but you should be spending more time with him if that is what he asks. That is just a simple example, but I believe you grasped the concept.

Many mothers do not receive praise from their boys because they may not be "praiseworthy," but what about the issue of the son who does not understand the value of giving praise? As I said, compliments seem to have gone the way of the cassette tape. For this boy, I recommend that you have him read Dale Carnegie's *How to Win Friends and Influence People*, after he reads my book of course.

Besides reading books, sit your son down and explain to him the importance of giving compliments. Explain to him the importance of thanking people for favors, and so on. Tell him how compliments impact a person's feelings, and explain that he can talk his way in and out of many situations when he knows the power of compliments. Explain to him that complimenting others builds rapport with his peers, and that skill will be very important when it comes time for him to look for a job or start a business or even get good grades in school.

The third reason I believe many mothers are not complimented is that their son's are just plain hardheaded. I do not believe that you can justifiably make this assumption until you first have made sure that you are worthy of receiving compliments, and second have taught your son the value of compliments. After you have done those two things and witness no improvement, you can rightfully say your boy is hardheaded.

My solution, which may or may not be feasible for you, but it will be effective, is to take your son to a convention of well-to-do folks, because this will allow him to see how prosperous, intelligent, and well-groomed grown men behave around one another. At this seminar or convention, your son can gain a different depiction of what a man is, other than the brute or overly-masculine man who never gives compliments that he may be used to seeing.

He will see how grown men, well respected men, greet each other, shake hands, compliment each others' attire, and give good pardons before meeting with the next acquaintance. Right now your son may be under the impression that compliments, thank yous and the like are weak or feminine, but showing him the other side of the story may open his eyes, and soften that hardhead of his.

Above all, do not give up on him. Give him time to change. It took me until I was 20…

How can you as a mother make yourself compliment worthy?
1. Ask your son what he expects from you and do the reasonable things he asks for that would make you a better parent.
2. Build a relationship where your son feels comfortable thanking you.
3. Possibly just do the opposite of what you have been doing up until now.
4. Try your best, do your best, work as hard or harder at home as you do at work.

If you do these things, you will make yourself compliment worthy. Even if your boy is hardheaded, he will look back on his life, as so many young men do,

THE GREATEST COMPLIMENTS

and realize that if not for his mother he would not have made it as far as he did. Then he will thank you.

Allow me to add that this will not only make you feel better as a mother when it all comes together, but imagine how much better of a man he will be for his future wife or next girlfriend when he understands how this principle works.

Chapter Twenty-four

Television and Other Influences: The Affects They Have on Your Son's Personality

When you learn to filter what goes into your mind, you keep your mind from clogging up with filth.

- Cederick W. Tardy II

I am not too sure that everyone knows or truly understands how fragile the mind of a young man can be, but a young man is one of the most self-conscious and frightened beings on the earth. Instead of externalizing that fear, young men tend to give off an air of confidence even though on the inside they are soft as bunnies, frightened by most everything. Your son is even more fragile than the bunny. He is like a little lion cub on the outside, prideful and fearless, but on the inside he is like a hummingbird. His mind is racing, he cannot stay still, and he is always looking for something.

The problem is that society has portrayed men as soldiers, fighters, and super men–confident and dashing. These are great characteristics for a man to have, but most men do not come equipped with these characteristics naturally; instead, most are acting them out. The older men are just better actors.

Your son has been taught to act by society. He has been taught to act out the same things that the older men have been taught. He feels as though he needs to have the character traits of the men he sees on TV. The problem with this is that those guys are actors. They are not real. Once the director screams "Cut!" those actors go back to being their regular selves, insecure and fearful. If you were to ask someone who really knew those actors, they would tell you about completely different sides of them than what they portray on TV. However, your son may not have this understanding yet. All he sees is that men respect those guys, girls love those guys, and society respects those guys. Naturally your son wants to be one of those guys.

As I said, the problem is that these people are actors, fakes. When your boy attempts to embody their TV traits, what is actually happening is that he is copying a fake. If you copy a fake you end up with a replica of a fake. This is where you as a mother need to step in. Don't let your son become a fake. Show him the types of men you really believe to be respectable. He is going to emulate someone, better let it be someone who you truly approve of. Show him what a true man looks like. Do not point him to men you find sexy, attractive, and smooth, unless you want a lot of baby mama drama.

Show him his culture, whichever culture that may be. In my case, my mother pointed me to my roots. African American mothers: Point your son to the strong black powerful leaders in history, and tell him that those should be his role models. When you do this, be sure to point out to him that the social war of the 60s is over, and he does not have to go around shouting "Black power." Make sure he knows that black men are good for more than music, dancing, football, basketball, and dying young in gunfire. Get some good influences in his life, because the truth is, he is almost definitely not going to do it on his own. He is going to gravitate towards society and fads. *As the planets revolve around the sun, your son will revolve around whatever gravitational force is pulling the hardest on him.* If you are tugging on him harder than society, he will lean towards you, but if society gets a hold of him, it will be hard to win him back.

Society pleases teens. The styles, cars, music, and even the food they eat are greatly influenced by society. Teens are victims to television and the music that follows. This is the main point I wish for you to understand. Teens are victims to the television images and the music images they see and hear. Most mothers do not understand this. They know it but do not understand it. They wonder why their kid can have everything he needs to succeed, but instead he throws it all away acting foolish like he witnessed someone do on TV. Remember, he does not understand that when the actor, rapper, singer gets done producing the movie or video they go back to their normal lives. Teenagers think those guys really live the lifestyle of girls, clubs, drinking, and partying all night long. They do not understand that it is all a ploy to get their 15 bucks at the CD store.

As plain as I can put it: Too many young black men are trapped in society's snare. Many have taken on a false and clownish image of who they think they are "supposed to be."

Look around at the styles, listen to the vernacular. Whatever styles are portrayed on BET and MTV become the instant fashion fad.

When your kid is at home with nothing to do, because no one is making him do his homework or plan for his future, he is watching these images over and over.

All he sees on TV is rapper after rapper with the girls he would die to have, and the clothes he would kill to wear, and all the money and fun he could desire.

He will begin acting out what he is seeing on TV and hearing on the CDs and radio. You wonder why he dresses like he does. You wonder why he speaks so crazily. You wonder why he walks like he does. It is all an attempt to be what he has let influence him for so long.

Anyone should be able to see where these influences have taken this generation. I had an acquaintance who had probably never shot a gun or been shot at, but he claimed all his scars were from gun battles. I can laugh about it now, knowing I used to be one of those guys, but it is not funny. This guy is lost. It may only be a phase. But, why let your son waste time on a phase that could become a lifestyle. The end will only result in wasted time. Time wasted cannot be regained. You, as his mother, need to be sure your child knows and understands this fact.

What is really important in life is helping others. Get him focused on what is important and do it early. Try not to wait until you feel comfortable about it. While you are trying to get comfortable, he is steadily falling deeper and deeper into the gravitational pull of society.

Educate your son on the truth. Make him proud to be an individual in a world full of copy cats. For my non-African-American audience, I know I am touching on a lot of African-American issues, but these things need to be said.

African-American single mothers, make your son proud to be black, but let him know what being black is. Make sure he understands being black is not a style. Let him know there are more ways for black men to make it in the world than selling drugs, dribbling a basketball, or rapping. Get a subscription to *Black Enterprise* magazine and show him what black people are doing in this world. Look up some of the current influential black people and show him what his culture is doing besides dribbling a basketball. Do not take his basketball away from him, because that would only cause strife. Just make sure he understands that he needs to focus on other alternatives for the future.

I believe that if you can put some positive influences in his path, it will make a big difference. It may not help or change things immediately, but it will plant that seed. Remember that a seed needs water to grow. You cannot plant a seed and then forget about it, because it will die. Plant that prosperity, business-minded, success-minded, overcoming-minded seed into him and water it. By water, I mean to continually repeat to him what you have said.

Education is the key to self-sustainability. Remember, the styles, trends, and fads are not the problem, it is the influences. *If your son's influences are off, his mind and thinking will be off.*

Chapter Twenty-five

Vision Chapter

The imagination allows us to see farther than the eye.

- Cederick W. Tardy II

It is time for you to start thinking about what you are going to do with everything you have read. It is time to get a vision.

A vision is a mental picture, image, or an idea that your inner eyes or imagination can see. A vision is the principle piece of a plan. This chapter is dedicated to enhancing vision, not by the use of eyeglasses, but by the use of pen and paper. What I want you to do here is write down the thoughts that come to you after reading each question. There is plenty of space below so be sure to use it all. Do not worry about what others will say about your visions. Your visions for your life and your son's life are your visions and not theirs.

Where do I see my family in one year?

_____

_____

Where do I see my family in three years?

_____

_____

Where do I see my family in five years?

_____

_____

Where do I see my family in ten years?

_____

_____

What do I want out of life in the next two years?

_____

_____

What do I want out of life in the next five years?

_____

_____

What are the things that I need to do to make all of these things a reality?

_____

_____

What would I have done different in the past? How can I implement those things into my present?

_____

_____

Where do I want to be financially in seven years?

_____

_____

What do I want from my son after he graduates high school?

_____

_____

What can I do to improve my current situation?

_____

_____

What resources (money, people, education, etc.) do I have available now that I am not using to their full extent?

_____

_____

Vision Chapter

Many people have never thought about their lives past tomorrow, next week, or next month. The majority of us tend to live life day by day, never truly giving thought to what is destined to come; the future. I was once told that the future is destined to come. That same influence told me that in order to have what I wanted in the future, I would need to start preparing for it now; in the present. I am proud to say that I have lived for the future for so long that my future preparations have now become my reality and my present.

Take the time to reread over the thoughts that you have written on the previous pages. I recommend transferring them into a Microsoft Word document. Read these thoughts consistently. Meditate on where you want to be in the next year, two years, three years, five years, 10 years, and even 20 and 30 years. The reality is that you will never have what you want if you do not plan and do what it takes to get it. Your reality, the life you are living right now, is a result of the amount of planning and preparation you put into it.

Those who choose to drift will find themselves tossed by the waves. Those who choose to study the ocean, build a boat, test the boat, enhance their boat, and then set out to sea may start the race long after those who jumped right into the water, but those who take the time to prepare make it to the finish line. Those who jump right in find out the ocean is much too big to travel without a plan or a map. Those who took time to study the ocean realized that the ocean was big way before they jumped in. The successful people in life do not rush into things, but instead they take time to prepare for them.

Start truly believing in the visions for your life that you have written. Soon, if you stick with them, your mind will begin to find ways and form ideas that will help bring those visions from imagination to reality.

The visions you have now may change over the years to come, but be sure that they never change for the worse. Never scale down your dreams. Especially never scale down your dreams because others tell you they cannot be done. *The limit is not the sky. The limit is your capacity to believe in yourself.* Choose to believe that the only thing that is impossible in this world is for someone to talk you out of what you believe. Believe in that with all your heart and you will succeed. I chose to tattoo that attitude on my brain. Occasionally things cause me to fail. Occasionally things cause me to reroute my original agenda, but circumstances never cause me to give up. The only impossible thing in this world is bringing down the determined individual.

Meditate and think intensely until those things you hope for, those things you've written become real in your imagination. When they become real in your imagination, you can then build a plan to bring them from your imagination to manifestation. It will take time. It will take patience. It will take sacrifice. Nothing grand was ever achieved without sacrifice.

Chapter Twenty-six

You Have to Believe

The exact moment you start to believe what you are doing is impossible is the exact moment that it becomes impossible.

- Cederick W. Tardy II

Believing in yourself and what you want to do is an important part of becoming successful. You will not succeed, you will not even try, if you don't believe. That is why the end of this book has been written to exhort, motivate, and encourage self-confidence. The exact moment that you doubt your son's ability to become anything more than a statistic is the exact moment you offer his life up to the statistics. You have to believe your son is better than that.

Believing is an unquestionable conviction in the object or idea of your focus. Mom, decide to unwaveringly trust in your son, even in the face of what the present circumstances are telling you. The moment he begins to doubt his significance, will be the exact moment he moves into the first turn in his downward spiral.

It is natural for humans to get downhearted from time to time, especially once we believe that no one believes in us. When no one believes in us, we lose faith in ourselves and begin to feel insignificant. It is an insignificant mindset that has a lot to do with the problems this generation is facing. It is the reason the suicide rate is climbing higher and higher. It is the reason teen pregnancy has become an epidemic. This insignificant mindset comes from having very little or no belief, no vision, low goals and no dreams.

Often times parents are the cause of their child's insignificant mindset. And often times, the parent has no idea. To avoid making your son feel insignificant you will need to refrain from talking to him as such and treating him as such. Simple fix right? That is the easy part. The hard part is realizing what things you say to him make him feel insignificant and damage his self-esteem. Your child is not an accident or sexual mishap. So you can't tell him those things. Your child, in your mind, has to be the greatest thing to ever walk this earth.

One of my acquaintances turned his life around during the time I wrote this book. Please hold your applause, because the most important part is what he told me when I saw him. This young man was at one point in time just as far gone as I ever was. His parents knew about his behavior, but since he was in his mid 20s, they let him live his life. When he told me he had changed for the better I was shocked. I asked him what his mother thought about him now that he had made steps in the right direction. His reply echoed in my ears.

He said, "I did not tell her. It does not matter what she thinks now. *It is a mother's job to always think highly of her son.*" As those words rattled in my brain, I replied, "So very true, but not too many do." We both got quiet for a few minutes as those thoughts rolled around in our brains. That conversation changed my entire outlook on parenting.

What do you think about the product of that discussion? Should a mother always be thinking highly of her son, whether he is on crack or walking a straight line? Your answer is all a matter of your personality, but I believe that he was absolutely right. A mother should always think highly of her son. If she doesn't who will? Will he? Without you believing highly in your son, it will be hard for him to believe in himself. Believing in your son is a principle and a principle is something that if used wisely will produce results.

If a mother tells her son with her words or actions that he is a good-for-nothing son, it really weighs heavily on his mind. Remember: A mother's words go right into her son's mind and heart.

Here is a question for you. Does an apple tree produce potatoes on the same branches as it does apples? Nope. Apple trees will never produce potatoes–unless someone scientifically mutates them to produce potatoes. The laws of nature say that everything will produce only after its own kind. This is important, because you are the tree. You are a tree mom, and you will only produce that which you are. If you are lazy, negative, and not willing to do what needs to be done to reach success, then you will only produce the same thing. That is the law of nature. Only when you begin to make changes in your life will you be able to change the things that you produce.

Here is another little sidebar: When you change, your friends, family, and co-workers should all be able to see a definite change in your behavior. Your child's teacher should be able to see a change in your behavior. Your child should be able to see a change in your behavior. Change is a visible thing. When I changed people saw it. I saw my friend as a new person when he changed. People should notice change. People who knew me before I changed see me differently now. That is just a pearl for those who are willing to embrace it and place it around their neck.

Belief is more than what you are talking. Belief is *expecting*. Expecting is trusting in the future, as you have imagined it. Expecting is making something happen because you believe that it has to happen. Your actions are the result of your beliefs. When you believe something has to happen, your belief will make you act accordingly to cause that thing to happen. When you believe something has to happen, it puts your mind in gear to make "it" happen.

If you believe that your son HAS to succeed, then your mind will get into gear to make that mental conviction a reality.

Many people can fool themselves or tell themselves that they believe in something when they really do not. People do it with risky investments all the time. This becomes an even greater danger when the false belief is in your son. I guarantee that if you do not truly believe in your son he will be able to notice and will resent you for it. Phony actions on your part will always turn him sour. You hate it when someone smiles in your face, but is thinking nasty things about you, and so does your son. Kids are not stupid. They can identify phony talk and phony actions very quickly.

Once you truly believe in your son without a doubt, you must pass that belief on to your son. I have offered a few things that you can use to transfer your belief to your son.

1. Mother-to-son talks: The number one thing you must know about a mother-to-son talk is that it is a one-way conversation, and that way is your way. This is when you sit him down in a chair, look him in the eyes, and sincerely tell him what is on your heart. I recommend the talk be of adequate length; five or 10 minutes is not enough, but hours and hours is too long. This is very effective on many levels, but the important thing is that it cements a lot more of what you say into your son's head than if you were just casually talking or ferociously yelling.

2. Repetitious proclamations: Tell him the same things repeatedly. You may have tried this with disciplining without great results I am sure, but it works a lot better when the message heard repetitively is positive and edifying. The more he hears a positive and encouraging message, the more chances that message has to become rooted in his thinking. It is like hearing a song. The first time you hear it you learn the melody, the second time you catch a little more. By the fifth time, you have a dance routine and are singing the words. Years later the song is implanted into your head, and you can recall the lyrics on command. That is how your advice, counsel, and guidance need to be.

3. Writing letters: Nothing tears down an impenetrable heart like a sincerely written letter. I recommend the letter to be handwritten, direct, and succinct. You can write as many letters as you would like, but soon your son may wonder why

You Have to Believe

you will not just talk to him face to face. Use letters when you are angry, have just gotten into an argument with your son, or are too uncomfortable to sit down and talk. You can hand deliver the letter or leave it in a place he will be sure to find it.

Do whatever works to make sure he knows you love and believe in him. You can use any of these three suggestions, and you could even combine them anyway you would like in order to reach your son's heart and mind.

Know this: The surest ways to a young man's heart and mind are through his eyes and ears. *If he does not want to listen you will have to reach him through his eyes.*

If you know your son will not read a letter or sit down long enough to listen to you, then you might be too late in trying to reach him, truthfully. If he is too far gone, there is only one thing that can help him and that is rock bottom. However, if he is not one of those who have to hit rock bottom to listen, then you must show him your belief in him.

Some of you might be thinking, "I have tried all of these things before and none of them worked." I say this, if you have tried a *principle* and it did not work for you then you did it wrong. Additionally, if you tried something and then quit, then you honestly did not believe that it was going to work before you tried it and that is where you failed. You missed step number one of any principle, which is believing in the principle unquestionably. You cannot try something for a short time and then when it does not work right away, give up and say it is foolishness. You cannot start working a principle with the mindset of, "I will try this, but if it doesn't work, I am going to quit." Just that mindset will ruin your conviction. Perform these principles persistently, and maintain them in action steadfastly for an extended period in order to see the expected results.

If you have tried to work a plan or strategy and it did not work out, you need to tailor make that plan for your specific situation. Just as a dress in a store might not fit you perfectly so you must tailor it to fit, you must do the same with the points in this book.

Take gold as another example. When a gold miner discovers gold ore, it does not look like it has any value. When someone first discovers gold, it looks like dirt. It is not until the gold is cleaned up and refined that it begins to have any value to the owner. The gold has to be shaped and molded to the owner's specifications before he or she can profit from it. The same thing goes with the strategies in this book. They are like little nuggets of gold that you must excavate, refine, mold, and shape to your specifications in order to profit from them.

Many times your kids go through life never really knowing how much you love and believe in them until it is too late. Nine times out of 10, your children do not understand the love a parent has for their child. It cannot even be comprehended by a child how much and in what way their parents love them.

How can your child recognize that you love him, especially if most of what you tend to say to him is pessimistic? Their brains do not think, "They are only trying to help. They love me. That is why they are correcting me." All their brains think is "*F* this and *F* that."

Your beliefs will affect their beliefs. If you look at your son and can only see a problem child, you will begin to speak nothing but those types of things toward him.

Begin to believe nothing but positives about your son, even when it is hard to do so, even when there is nothing positive in reality, because you will only treat him like you see him.

Have you ever noticed that when you use a public restroom that is clean you tend to do your best to keep it clean? You will try not to sprinkle water all over the counter. You will wash your hands and flush the toilet. On the other hand, if it is a nasty public restroom you treat it accordingly. You may not even wash your hands, you grab paper towels just to open the doors, and you then drop the paper towels on the ground because after all, everyone else did. You have the same type of thought patterns regarding your children. When you see them as a dirty restroom, you treat them like a dirty restroom. You may not want to, but on a subconscious level it is human nature. No one goes into a dirty restroom and treats it like a five-star resort facility. You believe that five-star facilities are better in every way so you treat them better in every way. You have to start seeing your kids as five-star young men. Right now your son may look like a dirty public restroom in your mind, but do not worry because there is mental bathroom cleaner, and it is called positive thinking!

Positive thoughts will clean up your negative mental outlook. The first few times you try to think positive thoughts about your boy it may be hard. You may try your best, but as soon as you finish a thought, you get a call from the principal saying your boy just got into another fight or something akin. This positive thought method works. Over time, the positive thoughts will produce a positive outlook and thought pattern. My mother had to do it for years.

I was on the wrong side of the track, but she believed in me. She kept hugging and kissing me, and telling me I was going to make it. She may have hated my guts as a person, but she loved me and believed in me as a son. No matter how many hurtful things I said that made her cry, she still loved me enough to think positively about me. She understood that positive thinking affects our believing, that our believing affects our actions, and that what we do affects our environment.

You Have to Believe

Life is choice driven, and our choices are created by our outlook on a circumstance. If your outlook is negative, your choice will be negative. It is so simple a process that it may seem like it will not work. I tell you it does. It may not work tomorrow. It may not work next week, but it will work.

My outlook started to change because my mother and stepfather began to look at me differently. I am now passing everything that I have learned in my straightening up down to you in this handbook in an attempt to say, "Parents, it is not too late for your children." Before you send them to a school for delinquents, try loving them unconditionally first. Yes, there are some kids who just will not get it until they are locked up in prison or down to their last dime, but *there are so many young people who will come around as soon as they get a vision for their future and know that someone believes that they can achieve that vision*. Most kids will come around once they realize someone believes in them, and that someone is counting on them.

I had no role models, but hey, the drug dealer thought I was cool enough to hang out with him. The drug dealer believed in me. He believed I could help him push drugs and make money. I believed in him because he believed in me, and we did what we set out to do. This is what happens. It may not be drugs. It could be anything. Something that does not line up with a path for success will take control of a child if they have no guidance.

I wrote a section in *A Head Start* that explains to your son the importance of finding and using a compass. The compass is not an actual compass, but *someone or something that will lead him in the right direction*. I instructed him to tell you where he wants to go in life. Now, I advise that you do not criticize him and beat him down if you do not like his initial dream. Remember that he is young, and he is likely to change his mind 50 times before the week is up.

One week my mother counted 21 things I told her I wanted to be when I grew up. She did not slap me and tell me I was stupid and weak minded. Instead, every instance she would say to me that my newest idea was a good choice, or if it was not, she would simply give me valid reasons why it wasn't a good choice. Encourage your kids to be whatever they want to be. Become their compass–someone or something that will lead him in the right direction. If you do not, someone else will. If the dream they have is out of your scope, then find someone for them that you know will be a good compass or role model for them. Above all else, just believe that no matter what, your son can and will be successful.

Do not look at him as a skinny little boy who is too clumsy to walk up the stairs without tripping. You need to envision the next leader of the community. Do not look at your son as a knucklehead, but as a prosperous pioneer. Your thoughts will produce your speech and your speech will produce your surroundings. Your son, as a youth, only has the potential to be what you groom him to be. He can only be what you expose him to.

I spoke to a person on my ship while I was in the Navy and just in that one meeting I think I could picture his parents. I asked him, "What would you do if you had a million dollars?" His reply was, "I do not know. That is too much money for me to even think about." He then gave me the saddest look I had seen on a human's face in a long time and walked out of my office. I turned to an acquaintance of mine and just kind of chuckled. It was not a normal chuckle though. It was one out of despair. I felt sorry for that young man. He had no will to think past one million dollars.

His parents must have never spoken vision and growth to him. I'm not saying that money is life, but if his parents didn't at least tell him to deposit his money into a bank and gain some sort of interest on it, then they also probably never told him he did not have to work for minimum wage all his life, or that he had the potential to be a success. His parents probably only showed him dollar stores and penny pinching.

That is all he was exposed to so that is all he knew. His imagination could not even give him a mental picture of what he would do with one million dollars. Isn't that sad? Even fools could say I would buy cars, boats, clothes, and watches. He could not even think that. All he could think was, "That is too much money." I believe he had no vision because his parents had no vision. You can be different though. You can give your son better vision. Not with Lens Crafters or Lasik, but by the words you speak and the things you expose him to in life.

You have to see success for him, and guide him to it until he can get there on his own. It is similar to teaching a child how to ride a bike. You have to show him how it works, and then you hold on to his seat and guide him. You try your best to keep them upright until finally they are riding off on their own.

This has been said over and over again, but this time you are going to get it from a "child's" perspective of how devastating it is. This is from my heart and soul. I shed tears of agony and tears of joy while writing this passage. I know you will be able to sense the emotion in the tone of this writing that was on my mind. That is because everything that happens in this world affects our minds. My mind was affected almost to the point of suicide because I felt like no one loved me. Take the things I have said throughout this book to your heart so you will never treat your kids this way or worse.

You have to believe in your son. You, no one else but you, his mother. If you do not believe in him, he will be less likely to believe in himself. *Most kids–most people–only need someone to believe in them and count on them for them to get their heads into the game.* Trust me.

Conclusion

Live every day as if it is the last day to teach your child the things he will need to know in order to succeed in life.

- Cederick W. Tardy II

So there you have it. *The Big Payback*. What did you think?

I hope you were not disappointed. Now go hug your son. Hug him like you never have before.

I will quit with this last tidbit: *Everyone in this world has challenges. We have to decide whether to overcome those challenges or succumb to them. Aim high at all times! But aim with precision.*

As promised, here is my contact information for any questions, comments, concerns, testimonies, or just to say hello or thank you.

The Web site: www.ctardyenterprises.com

Send e-mails to: cederick@ctardyenterprises.com

Mailing Address:

The Big Payback
P.O. Box 840654
Houston, TX 77284

Connection Questions

Below are seven groups of questions that you can have a sit down talk with your son regarding. The questions refer to the books that you both have just completed, as well as the future that you both will inevitably endure. Answer the questions mutually. Each question is designed to connect the two of you on a project.

Seven Questions

1. What are we going to do now with the knowledge that we have gained? What steps will we take? What direction do we want to go and how will we get there?
2. Do our visions written in the vision chapters coincide with one another's? What does? What doesn't? Can we reach a mutual agreement on our visions?
3. What topics did your book cover that mine didn't? Can any of the information help me?
4. What five points had the greatest impact on you and why? What were the best points that you underlined or highlighted?
5. If we could redo the last five years of our lives together with the knowledge we have now after reading these books, what would we do differently?
6. What do you think will hinder us from building a strong relationship together? What can we do to prevent those hinderances from having control over our lives?
7. What can I do to help you become a better person?

Epilogue

We are so individually important that the God who created this world and the entire universe is willing to listen to our prayers.

- Cederick W. Tardy II

Has anyone ever tried to talk to you about becoming a Christian? *That was God knocking.* Has your heart ever felt like something was missing, and you knew it was God, but you ignored that feeling? *That was your heart trying to answer His knock.*

There is a real God who loves you enough to give you chance after chance, day after day, month after month, to find your way back to Him. Answer that knock. Open your door to Him. Let Him live in your dwelling.

Many call themselves Christians because they thank God for a Grammy Award and so forth. We have all seen the man or woman, who you know for a fact is, well… isn't, at the least, trying to live their life for God. But they stand up on stage and thank God for their award or accomplishment. I am not expressing contempt toward these people. I just do not want to be an "on stage Christian."

You all have just finished reading about my life. You know where I have come from. Thank God that He is merciful. I am not a perfect man. I am not a pastor. I am not even a flawless Christian. But, I know I would be wrong if I did not offer everyone who has read this book a chance to receive salvation as I have. The fear of hell turned my life around. You may not believe in heaven or hell, but like I always say, "Why take that chance?" Salvation is free. All you have to do to receive salvation is speak out, believe, and be saved.

Romans 10:9-10 says, "If you confess with your mouth, 'Jesus is Lord,' and believe in your heart that God raised him from the dead, you will be saved. It is with your heart that you believe and are justified, and it is with your mouth that you confess and are saved."

The following prayer is a general prayer of salvation. If you are willing, pray this prayer out loud, with a sincere heart. You may not feel any different afterwards, which may have you thinking it was a waste of time, but trust me it isn't. My life changed for the better the moment I truly committed my life to serving the Father and helping His children.

Pray this prayer aloud

Dear God, I know and believe that without Jesus and Your Word in my life I am lost. Father I do not want to go to hell. I know that I have broken your laws and sinned, but I want to turn away from my sinful life. I want to know You. I do not know all the scriptures right now Father, but I know and believe that without Jesus I am lost. I want to answer Your knock. I believe that Jesus died on the cross and paid the penalty for my sins and mistakes. I believe Romans 10:9-10 which says that if I receive Jesus as the Lord of my life I can be saved. Thank You, Father. I believe that I am now a part of the Family of God and that You are my Heavenly Father. Please help me obey You so that I can do Your will for the rest of my life. Father God, thank You for saving me. Jesus, I thank You for sacrificing Your life so that I may live. In Jesus' name, I pray. Amen.

Welcome to the family! If you have prayed the prayer of salvation and meant it, you are now a follower of Jesus. I encourage you now to find a local church where you can be baptized and grow in the knowledge of God through His Word, the Bible. *Be patient with yourself.* Find a "good" church home, one that teaches the Word and not preaches the Word. Get hooked up with people who are doing their best to walk and talk as Christians seven days a week. Taking the time to learn who God truly is will be the best decision you ever make.

Promotion Page

Book Ced

The transformation that I went through is nothing short of amazing. Today I draw on my experiences to help single mothers and youths transform their own lives through my public speaking efforts. If you would like to have me speak to your organization or know of an organization that would benefit from my message, please visit my Web site at www.ctardyenterprises.com and look for the BOOK CED tab. There you will find my schedule and an easy request form to fill out or e-mail me directly at cederick@ctardyenterprises.com.

Upcoming Book

Stay on the look out for my next book titled, *"What Father's Should Be Telling Their Daughters!"* This is a book you will not want to miss.

The target audience is young girls, preteens to young teens. The purpose is to enlighten their minds on many subjects pertaining to life and the pursuit of a better one.

While the book is targeted to young girls, the content is beneficial for mothers and fathers as well.

You will want to stay glued to the Web site and sign up for the periodic newsletter to stay up to date on the completion of this work.